GREAT WESTERN RAILWAY

TRAVELLING POST OFFICES

BY

J. G. HOSEGOOD

WILD SWAN PUBLICATIONS LTD.

ISBN No. 0 906867 16 9

Designed by Paul Karau
Typesetting by Berkshire Publishing Services
Photo reproduction and offset plates by Oxford Litho Plates Ltd.
Printed in Oxford

Published by
WILD SWAN PUBLICATIONS LTD.,
Hopgoods Farm Cottage, Upper Bucklebury, Berks.

INTRODUCTION

IN the blackness of the night, the signalman, in his oasis of light and warmth, pulls off the levers to herald the approach of another train. Above a cold, damp and empty platform the signal arm drops and the steady glow of the forbidding red lamp changes to green. Quietly out of the rain and wind the Travelling Post Office soon arrives and draws to a halt shrouded in steam. It is met by a team of postmen and porters with swaying lamps, their heavy coats blown open by the prevailing wind. With a dull thud and tinkle of buckles, the heavy bags of mail are exchanged and wheeled away. A few words are exchanged with those standing in the light of the carriages before the doors close and in the same quiet way the ghost train's red tail lamp slides away down the platform into the night, slowly disappearing from the now empty platform while the signal returns to its steadfast red.

So passed the train which appeared on no passenger timetable, was seldom seen and yet whose contents were awaited by everyone.

Such was the passing of the TPO whose closed doors still hide a secret world of their own rarely seen by the passing passenger – an essential part of a system by which afternoon mail posted in London can be delivered to the correct address in any part of Great Britain the following morning. The security, odd hours of work and limited numbers of these vehicles has only added to their aura of mystery, further aided by the few photographs and general lack of information about them.

Perhaps the most famous of these trains was the Great Western Travelling Post Office, often affectionately referred to as 'the Great West'. This almost unique service was only outranked by the Up and Down Special and the North West TPOs from Euston. For six nights a week the '10.20 postal' was loaded under the great arches of Brunel's Paddington station. The train, comprising a mixture of special vehicles designed for stowage, sorting of letters and parcels, had a set formation: three sorting vans manned by 34 staff, three letter stowage vans and four parcel stowage vans for Bristol, Exeter, Plymouth and Penzance. It departed with over a thousand mail bags for sorting and delivery to stations en route such as Reading, Bath, Bristol, Taunton, Newton Abbot, Plymouth, Saltash, St. Austell, Truro, Redruth, Hayle and Penzance. Bags were exchanged while the train was on the move with special apparatus at Maidenhead, Chippenham and Liskeard, but there were always bags for exchange with the other TPOs such as the South Wales TPO with which 'the Great West' connected at Bristol.

The operation was carried out with ordered precision, and stowing the bags on board was far from the shambles and chaos that it may have appeared to the onlooker. 'Made-up' bags for various destinations were arranged in the stowage vans in strict rotation. Others requiring attention were put ready for the sorters and one by one each of the sacks was emptied and sorted into the racks of pigeon holes which lined the sorting coach. When the hole was full, the bundles were placed in the appropriate mail bag, hanging Christmas stocking fashion on the opposite carriage side wall. When each was full or complete it was sealed and labelled and returned to the stowage van. Cryptic abbreviations conveyed to the initiated all the information needed to complete the delivery.

It was a race against time all through the night to get the mails ready for their destination, timed to within seconds when the mail exchange apparatus was in use. The exchange was a tricky operation as the postman had to know exactly where and when the apparatus was to be worked. He could not just rely on the time as the engine driver might be making up time before or after a permanent way slack. He had to recognize the location from the sequence of sounds reflected from the lineside as the train made its approach to the point. To put the apparatus down too early might mean damage to the coach or the lineside fittings. At Liskeard, for instance, the traductor arms had to be lowered after the station platform was passed. What might be collected from the platform in the net in the form of porters, passengers, platform trolleys and other railway paraphernalia is best imagined. On some of the northern TPOs the exchanges were so close together that the crews had to work at breakneck speeds to be ready in time to make the exchanges.

Accidents did occur although fortunately they were few and far between. If the train was travelling too slowly the bags could fly over the net and remain hanging on the standards. Bags being dispatched are even known to have passed up through the ground net, break open and scatter their contents along the lineside. Rumour even has it of a bag flying into a canal followed by the postman attempting a recovery!

All the time a careful tally was kept of the bags received and despatched and the thickening wallet of chits marked the progress of the train.

Bristol was the interchange point for the 'Great West' TPO. Here both the 'up' and 'down' TPOs met to connect with the South Wales TPOs to and from Carmarthen and the Derby-Bristol and return TPO, mails from these and other TPOs being interchanged as required. On the 'down' 'Great West' some of the sorters left the train to travel back to London with the 'up' service, the bulk of the sorting having been completed, while the rest carried on towards the West Country. At Plymouth more left while some local men joined for the final haul into Cornwall and Penzance. The sorting was completed to such an extent that the Penzance mail was virtually sorted into the postman's rounds!

The actual task of sorting is still very skilled, requiring a high standard of fitness and stamina, very good eyesight and quick physical and mental reactions. When considering the long hours worked without a break in the confined noisy and uncomfortable conditions, with rigid time schedules, it seems remarkable that such high standards were maintained. Early TPOs were poorly lit by gas and most were not even equipped with lavatories! Each individual envelope or packet is picked up, scanned and sorted into the correct pigeon hole in a practically unbroken movement, but when pigeon holes often have no markings, a sorting rate of 50 to 70 letters a minute is extremely good going.

And so away into the night passes the mobile sorting office, travelling at high speed, bringing mails from one end of the country to the other in coaches specially built and equipped for the operation. Such has to be the availability of the coaches that in many cases a spare is provided for the service. The GW TPO throughout its history has always had three sets of coaches, one in use on the 'down', one on the 'up' and a third spare set which usually stands by at Old Oak Common, 'resting'. This also allows for vehicles receiving works attention, as it is of primary importance that the mails should go through on time, and not be hindered by lack of rolling stock.

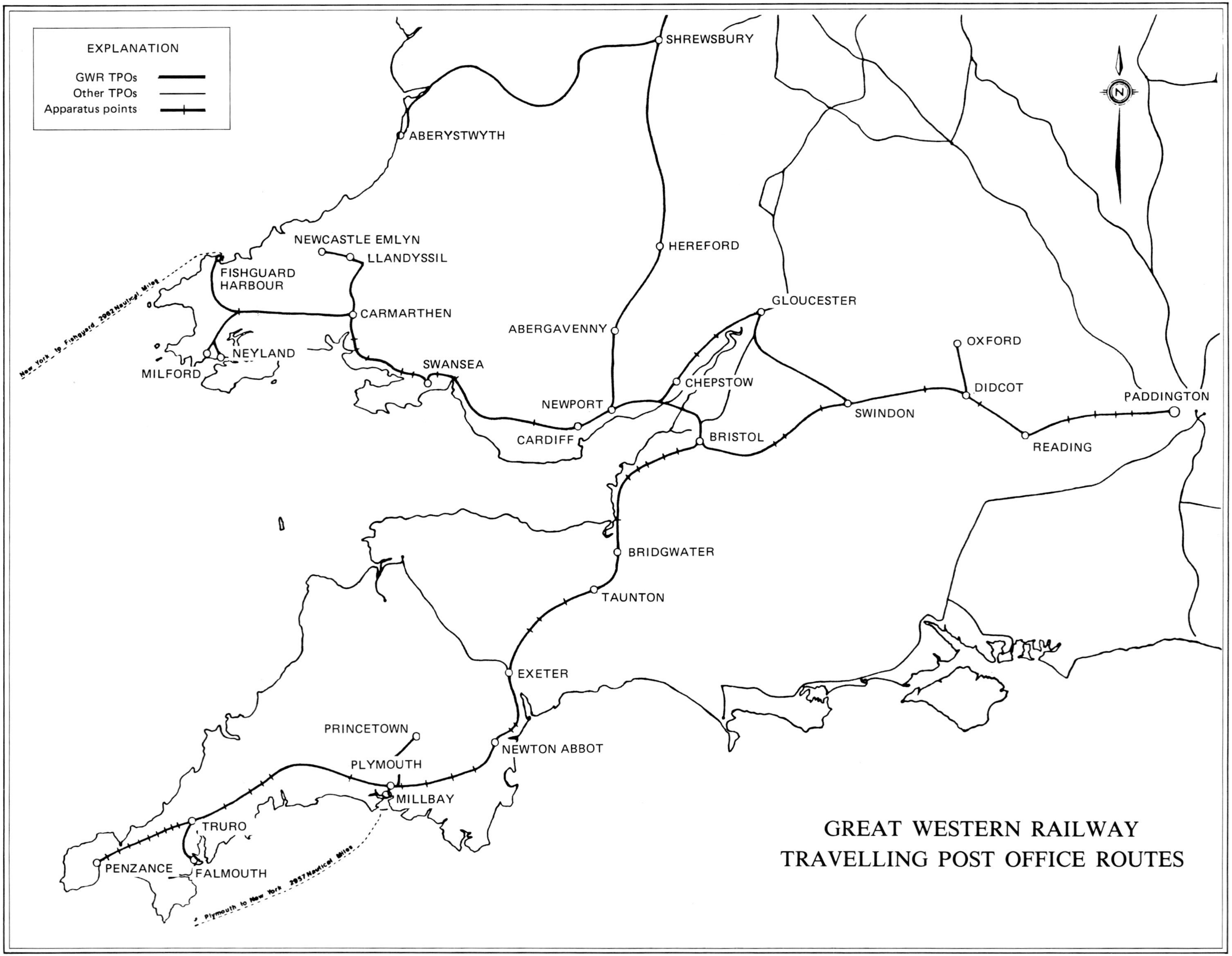

GREAT WESTERN RAILWAY
TRAVELLING POST OFFICE ROUTES

CHAPTER ONE

THE SERVICES

To trace the early history of the mail services of the Great Western Railway is almost to trace the advancement of the railway itself. Previously the mails were carried by the 'Posting Coaches' which left London for all parts of the country.

The Post Office lost no time in switching the conveyance of mails to the railways and by 1830 letters were being carried by the Liverpool & Manchester Railway. This is understandable when the condition of many of the roads is taken into account. In the early 1800s the London mail coach could not operate past Shrewsbury, while in Anglesey the road was so bad that it scarcely deserved the status, apparently being nothing more than a miserable track! It was in 1808 that the Post Office attempted to run a mail coach through to Holyhead without much success, and the roads of the West of England were not much better. The state of the turnpikes depended upon the finances of the trust responsible for each section and in turn the population and traffic of the locality. Hence the further west from London, the worse the roads became.

A vast number of road surveys were completed between 1815 and 1830 but, with the advent of the railways, most of these plans were forgotten. Thomas Telford, in 1808, began his survey of the Holyhead Road, but it was not until 30th January 1826 that the 'Royal London and Holyhead Mail' coach was able to make a through journey on the opening of the Menai Bridge, one of the first suspension bridges in the world. Seven months later the Holyhead to Chester Mail was to pass through by the Conway suspension bridge opened on 1st July 1826.

In 1823 the Postmaster General again engaged Thomas Telford to survey and improve the route for the South Wales part of the London–Bristol–Milford Irish Mails. The New Passage Ferry, where several important mail contracts crossed the River Severn, was described by Telford as 'one of the most forbidding places at which an important ferry was ever established'.

Little transpired from the surveys made by Henry Welch and Joseph Mitchell, both working under the direction of Thomas Telford in South Wales. None of his recommendations, which included the building of a suspension bridge over the River Severn at Beachley, was accepted. With the advent of the railways, the mail coaches stood little chance of survival.

POSTAL HISTORY

Sir Rowland Hill, as he was to become, brought about a total change to the postal system where payment had depended upon distance, with complex rates and anomalies. The recipients, who were responsible for paying for carriage, often had to refuse delivery as they could not afford the costs.

This often forgotten Victorian inventor was born the third of six sons of a brass foundry manager, at Kidderminster in December 1795. In his lifetime he invented a pendulum device for measuring time, improved steamboat propulsion and developed the rotary printing press. As a schoolmaster he developed the school as it is seen today with separate classrooms, laboratories, gymnasium and libraries.

His great ambition was the introduction of a postal system based on the uniform pre-paid delivery system. His plans were described by his critics as unworkable, but through the support of Queen Victoria the famous Penny Post was introduced in May 1840. He also improved the manufacture of envelopes and supported Anthony Trollope in advocating roadside postal boxes. His stamps, the Penny Black and the Twopenny Blue, were to become world famous.

The Penny Post covered letter mail but there was still no agreement to adopt a uniform pre-paid system for parcels and in 1842 there were three systems of letter and parcel post in use.

With the introduction of the uniform letter post, a number of railway companies had received mail contracts in which payment was based upon the weight of mail irrespective of the distance it was carried. The second system involved the payment of a toll to the railway company for the carriage of mail, while in the third the railway acted as carriers and charges were related to both the distance and weight of the article. The GWR added to this confusion by making additional charges according to the train that the packet was carried upon, a rather irksome arrangement which was very unpopular with traders.

Sir Rowland Hill's pressure for a parcel post was dismissed by the Treasury in 1842 as impracticable. The establishment and acceptance of a parcel post became a forty year battle and today it is still possible to forward parcels by numerous carriers, including the Post Office and the railways.

The year 1853 saw the introduction of the book post by which parcels of books could be sent in open-ended packets through the post for a charge of 6d per pound weight. The failure of the Post Office and the railway companies to extend the principles of letter post, together with a deterioration in service in the early 1850s, encouraged a large number of independent carriers to circumvent the high charges of the railway companies for the conveyance of 'smalls'. The cost of sending a single consignment of small items was far less than sending them individually. Large hampers would therefore be sent to one point to be broken down by an agent, thus effecting a considerable economy.

In 1863, in an effort to break the deadlock, the Post Office introduced the 'sample post' whereby samples could be sent at a much reduced rate. It had been this type of traffic which had suffered under the 'smalls' system. However, the railway Traffic Superintendents complained that they were making a loss on small packets and that half of the items sent by this method were not samples at all. The following year the railways had reduced their rates to conform with the Post Office for parcels by passenger train, but on distances of over 300 miles the Post Office was still cheaper. Although the sample post was abolished on 5th October 1871, the Post Office still offered cheaper rates than the large railway companies. Consequently much discussion took place between the various companies in an effort to reduce the rates in line with the Post Office and give the Post Office unfettered control of parcels traffic in a similar way to the letter post. On 1st August 1883 a cheap parcels post was introduced based on the uniform charge

An artist's impression of an early TPO coach as used on the London & Birmingham Railway, with an early style receiving net.

concept adopted by the letter post forty-three years before. Greater quantities of parcels traffic were therefore carried by the Travelling Post Offices operated solely for the Post Office, instead of the railway companies' own systems and services.

RAILWAY DEVELOPMENTS

The slow speeds associated with the early tramroads, which were of a local nature, had held no inducement to the Post Office to divert traffic. Speed was essential and Sir Rowland Hill had even considered a scheme for having a horse-drawn mail coach fitted with sorting boxes for use by the mail guard while still en route. However, although the mails were arriving in London at 6.00 am and distribution did not commence until 9.00 am, his suggestion was not adopted.

With the increased speed the railways offered over the posting coaches, even with improved roads, the mails soon took to the railways. The advantages of the new transport system became evident with the opening of the Liverpool and Manchester Railway on 15th September 1830, the first mail traffic by rail being taken between Liverpool and Manchester on 11th November.

In anticipation of the opening of the Grand Junction Railway on 4th July 1837 the Post Office despatched mails from London on the 3rd. These were taken to Birmingham by coach and thence to Liverpool and Manchester by rail. The service proved effective and around 740 bags a day were being transferred by rail in September of that year. The first Travelling Post Office, consisting of a converted horse-box temporarily fitted as a sorting coach, commenced running on 6th January 1838 between Birmingham and Liverpool. The experiment proved so successful that on 19th June TPOs became a permanent part of postal arrangements.

The first specially constructed TPO sorting coach appeared in 1838. It was 16 ft long and built for the Grand Junction Railway Company at a cost of £600. Although the service had only just started, the carriage was fitted with apparatus for receiving and despatching mails at speed.

The first TPO from London was run before the entire length of the London & Birmingham Railway was completed. It ran from London to Denbigh Hall, north of Bletchley, where the old coach road of Watling Street was crossed by the railway. Passengers and parcels were conveyed to the next section of the line at Rugby in coaches belonging to the famous coaching partners, Chaplin & Horne.

On the completion of the Kilsby Tunnel, the railway was opened throughout its length on 17th September 1838, so joining the Grand Junction Railway and the North Union Lines for a direct route to the north. The Post Office, looking for a rational system of through communications, wrote to Richard Creed, the Secretary of the London & Birmingham Railway, on 24th September 1838, requesting the TPO to be run through from London to Warrington direct. The London & Birmingham directors agreed and the necessary arrangements were made the following day.

On 1st July 1839 the GWR extended its service from Paddington as far as Twyford, the limit of the line at this time, but it was not until December that year that any records occur of mails being carried on a regular basis. The actual date upon which the GWR first carried mail is a little obscure and may well have been a local arrangement. It was certainly before December 1839. The GWR were the first to introduce a night mails service on 4th February 1840 when the 8.55 p.m. carried the mail for Bath, Bristol, Stroud and Gloucester.

By July 1841 the GWR had completed their line through to Bristol and the Post Office requested the company to supply four bag tenders for use on the 'Night Mail' and four partially converted second class coaches for the 'Day Mail'. The former were built under the direction of Sir Daniel Gooch.

The June 1844 timetable opposite gives the timings for these trains, the sorting on which was initially restricted to between Bristol and Exeter for towns as far west as Devonport. This was later extended to include mails on the Falmouth and Bude lines and brought about the extension of the bag tenders through to Exeter. Brunel was very much in favour of concentrating on the mail traffic from Plymouth and reached an agreement with the London & South Western Railway who consequently carried the majority of the liner passengers while the GWR carried the mails. This agreement was eventually to lead to a tragic disaster at Salisbury.

The first serious railway mail theft was on the Great Western in 1849 when two men of respectable appearance purchased first class tickets from Laira to Bristol, travelling next to the Post Office coach. They rifled the mails prior to Bridgwater, leaving the train at Bristol. A passenger tipped off the authorities and two men were arrested.

Long before the arrival of the railways, robbing the mails was a common occurrence and punishable by death. The last man to be hanged for this was executed on 13th February 1835, the death penalty for the offence being removed in 1872. In one week in 1813 the *Bristol,* the *Telegraph* and the *Expedition* coaches were all robbed. In 1827 the *Warwick* mail was robbed of £27,000, a huge sum for those days.

Initially the custom of the mail being entrusted to a mail guard, as practised on the posting coaches, was continued, but by 1848 arrangements were made for the mail bags to be left in the charge of the train guard. Post Office sorters were first employed on TPOs on 5th May 1857 when five men were selected to work a system of District Sorting Carriages between London and Crewe on the LNWR.

Life on the early TPOs was extremely hazardous with serious accidents and danger to life all part of the job. Few

1844 TIMINGS

		Day Mail				Night Mail	
Paddington	dept.			10.15		8.55	
	arr.		8.20		1.10		4.50
Bristol	dept.	9.20			8.35		00.25
	arr.			2.35		1.45	
Exeter	dept.		12.45				9.35
	arr.	12.05				4.05	

could bear the wear and tear of the Travelling Post Office for more than fifteen years! Between 1860 and 1867 there were twenty-eight accidents in which TPO men were seriously injured or killed. Fumes from the oil lamps and wax used for sealing the bags caused nausea and affected the brain, which was the cause of a large number of early retirements from paralysis, nervous debility and mental derangement. Things have improved with the TPO now having one of the best accident records in the Post Office. Nowadays TPO staff are all volunteers from London and the twenty-two provincial centres throughout Great Britain, and all travelling staff are Postmen 'Higher Grade'. Previously postal staff were divided into seniors and juniors, known as railway clerks, and in addition on the early TPOs a number of mail guards were also employed to take charge of all bags. They were responsible for despatches and receipts at stations and apparatus points.

THE SERVICES

The Post Office required the railway companies to provide an efficient service with regular trains running to time. However, such was the state of the railways in 1854 that a House of Commons committee had been set up to investigate the poor services given by the railway companies. The outcome of a consequent meeting between Sir Rowland Hill and Saunders, the Secretary of the GWR, was the running of a 'Special' train for the exclusive use of the Post Office. The 'Special' commencing on 1st February 1855, consisted of two sorting vans and a stowage van, which ran from Paddington to Bristol with the West of England and the South Wales mails. On arrival at Bristol it was split, with some vans continuing on a passenger train to Exeter. It was officially called the 'Special Mail' but became known to the staff as the 'Little Mail'.

The use of the term 'special' to TPOs means that the train is a complete TPO and carries no other traffic or passengers, being run solely for the Post Office. The 'Special Mail' was the only special TPO on the GWR/WR and became the 'Great Western TPO'. All other TPOs ran to the Post Office time requirements but carried other traffic and often passengers.

District Sorting Carriages were introduced in 1857 to lessen the work in the main London offices in sorting and making up bags for provincial centres. On the DSC mail was sorted and bagged for the main centres along its route, leaving detailed sorting to the centre concerned. On the 'up' journey the bags were sorted and made up into the ten postal districts of London introduced in 1857. The DSCs proved to be very expensive to operate and were withdrawn in 1869.

Sunday Sorting Tenders were introduced following Sir Rowland Hill's wish to reduce the amount of sorting required on Sundays in London's main offices. They ran in 'down' trains on Saturday nights and picked up mail from places too close to London to be sorted on the 'up' direction. At first the mail travelled in the wrong direction away from its destination, being sorted and then transferred to the TPOs in the 'up' direction. Since 1904 the Sorting Tenders have been known as Sorting Carriages, under the control of the London TPO section. Today there are only three Sorting Carriages and these are all in Scotland.

From time to time, especially near the Christmas period, additional TPOs have been run, as in 1913 for instance when vast amounts of mail were sent to Exeter to relieve other offices. Once sorted, the mails were sent from Exeter by a special TPO departing at 1.00 p.m. for Bristol and London. This train could best be described as a bag tender, which has a present day parallel when just before Christmas all TPOs are suspended and run as bag tenders with no sorting and no late fee posting facility.

The contract between the Post Office and the GWR remained virtually unchanged from its inception, the first lasting for five years, commencing on 23rd June 1844. The value of the contract progressively rose but only the number and timings of the mail trains were subject to alteration. The contract covered the running of mail trains which the GWR could use for passenger traffic at the Post Office's convenience and timings. The running of these trains was not always to the times laid down by the Post Office who reserved the right to require the GWR to run a special in its place. The GWR had to provide, maintain and replace the carriages required for the TPO services all of which had to be fitted out to the requirements of the Inspector General of Mails, who inspected them prior to their use. Any alterations required once the carriages were approved were at the Post Office's own expense. Employees of the GWR were expected to assist with the loading and unloading of the mails at the stations along with the Post Office's

Warlock, a broad gauge 'Rover' class 4–2–2 speeds the 'up' North Mail past Exminster in May 1891. The leading coach is an unidentified broad gauge TPO equipped with exchange apparatus. *Warlock* was one of two 'Rovers' shedded at Newton Abbot at this time. *Rev. A. H. Malan*

Acceleration of the Night Mail to and from Cornwall, and of the North Mail to South Wales.

THE Postmaster-General has made arrangements with the Great Western Railway Company for accelerating the Mails above mentioned on and from the 1st March.

CORNWALL.

The Night Mail will reach—

Liskeard	... at 5.18 a.m.	... ...	12 m.	Earlier than at present,
Truro ...	... „ 6.29 „	... ...	16 m.	
Falmouth	... „ 7. 2 „	... ...	13 m.	
Penzance	... „ 7.35 „	... ...	35 m.	

and will be despatched from—

Penzance	... at 5. 0 p.m.,	1 hr. 10 m.	Later than at present.
Falmouth	... „ 5.25 „	0 hr. 50 m.	
Truro ...	... „ 6. 3 „	0 hr. 48 m.	
Liskeard	... „ 7.25 „	0 hr. 40 m.	

At other Towns and in Rural districts dependent thereon, a proportionate improvement will be effected.

SOUTH WALES.

The North Mail will reach—

Newport	... at 6.28 a.m.,	0 hr. 47 m.	Earlier than at present,
Cardiff ...	... „ 6.49 „	0 hr. 51 m.	
Swansea	... „ 8.42 „	1 hr. 23 m.	
New Milford	„ 11.40 „	1 hr. 15 m.	

and by the use of a Travelling Sorting Office in the Train from Gloucester westward, the delivery of letters at the chief places on the route will be still further accelerated.

BY ORDER.

GENERAL POST OFFICE,

February, 1884.

Printed for Her Majesty's Stationery Office by W. P. GRIFFITH & SONS, Prujean Square, Old Bailey, London, E.C.

'Rover' class 4–2–2 *Bulkeley* at Didcot with an 'up' broad gauge day mail. The two leading coaches are narrow-bodied stock on broad gauge underframes, this being particularly evident on the TPO coach where the traductor arms have been set out onto the broad gauge underframes in order to maintain the correct clearances with the ground apparatus. *L & GRP, courtesy David & Charles*

personnel, while the Post Office were required to deliver the mail in bags to the stations in reasonable time for the train. The times of many branch line trains were arranged to connect with the controlled trains in speeding the mails to their destinations.

Services were divided into three schedules, the first of which covered the running of the TPOs. The times of these trains were laid down in the contract and could only be altered by the Post Office. The second schedule covered the running of the various secondary trains and those of the branch lines to meet with the TPOs, upon which mail was to be forwarded. The third part of the schedule covered the Post Office's use of any GWR train, although the use of the company's buses and ships was not expected and never fell within the contracts. Provisions were to be made at all stations for separate rooms to be made available for postal use and the Post Master General took powers to erect and maintain lineside apparatus, something which the GWR were very unhappy about.

For this service and the privilege of carrying the mails, the Post Office initially, in 1840, paid the GWR five guineas per day for four mail trains with the figure steadily rising as the years progressed and the services expanded.

These payments were frequently the source of troubles between the railway companies and the Post Office, often ending with arbitration as with the claim of £27,140 14s. 0d. paid to the Bristol & Exeter Railway for the services between 6th January 1850 and 15th December 1853. The railway company had asked for between £50,000 and £60,000 as during this period the mails had been conveyed an estimated 55,480 miles in the sorting tender coaches provided by the Company. The Post Office seems to have expected value for money to a staggering degree.

CHANGE OF GAUGE

The GWR had been built to two gauges, that of the broad gauge and, as the GWR terms it, the narrow gauge or standard gauge. The GWR's adoption of the broad gauge had been at the insistence of Brunel who believed that the wider the gauge the better the riding qualities available. The standard gauge had no logical thought behind it, having come from collieries of Northumberland, and in the laying of the Stockton & Darlington line (1821-1825) George Stephenson had seen no reason to depart from the previously adopted gauge. In ignoring Brunel's reasoned planning, the railways have suffered ever since. The GWR were to be left out in the cold by all the other railways who adopted the standard gauge, mostly due to the additional cost of the extra width.

Broad gauge lines were eventually converted to mixed gauge and a steady changeover to the narrow gauge took place until the final conversion in May 1892. Apart from a number of coaches which needed conversion, the GWR had the problem of keeping the TPO operation running while the gauge change was completed. The conversion of the West of England lines required the stoppage of all trains during the alterations, but the Post Office would not tolerate any interruptions to the TPOs without considerable compensation from the GWR. The mail trains therefore played an important part in both the final hours of the broad gauge and the first of the narrow gauge. The last broad gauge passenger train to depart from Paddington was the 5.00 p.m. to Plymouth, hauled as far as Bristol by 'Rover' class 4–2–2 *Bulkeley* and on to Newton Abbot by *Iron Duke*. This train crossed the 'Up Night Mail' at Teignmouth, the last occasion on which two broad gauge trains crossed. *Bulkeley* returned from Bristol to Paddington with the 'Up Night Mail' the following morning, arriving at 5.30 a.m., some one and a half hours late. This was the last broad gauge arrival at Paddington. The loco and stock was then worked back to Swindon to be stored prior to conversion.

The broad gauge stock was stored in additional siding accommodation laid in the vicinity of the station reservoir, at a cost of £5,000, and further sidings built on land purchased to the east of the Gloucester branch at an approximate cost of £250 per acre. Further stock had also been stored on the Brentford branch.

The 'Down Night Mail' of the 29th May was a narrow gauge train diverted over the South Western's line between

Exeter and Plymouth, an arrangement which continued during the following two nights. On 30th and 31st the morning mails and passengers for Cornwall were carried from Plymouth Millbay Docks to Fowey and Falmouth by a steamer, which returned in the afternoon, connecting with the 'Up Mail' which ran via the South Western's route to Exeter. Such was the planning of the gauge conversion that the narrow gauge 'Night Mail' from Paddington on the Sunday was booked to depart from Plymouth for Penzance, following the conversion at 4.00 a.m.

The South Wales area had already been converted in 1872, the last broad gauge train leaving South Wales on 11th May hauled by *Brunel*. Mail trains again dominated the arrangements, the first narrow gauge train being the 12.50 a.m. 'Down Night Mail' from Gloucester the following morning. The first 'up' train was the 'Up Mail' departing Milford at 4.00 p.m. No crossing places had been provided on the route during conversion such that the initial services were only in a single direction. Coaching stock for this service was not from the 'down' service as might be expected but from Swindon via Oxford, Worcester, Hereford and Neath, where it had been stored until required.

The last train between Cheltenham and Swindon, via Gloucester was the 'Up Midnight Mail' although some empty coaching stock and locomotives followed early on the morning of 26th May. The first 'down' narrow gauge train was the 'Down Night Mail' on the Sunday night.

LATE LETTER SERVICE

One of the facilities of the TPOs is the ability to post letters onto the train at a far later time than any of the normal collections. It is still possible to post a letter from Bristol at 00.30 a.m. and for it to receive first delivery in London. At first the public could hand letters direct to the mail guard without paying a fee, but in 1860 a late fee of 2d was introduced. Later in 1880 this was reduced to ½d at which figure it remained until 1969 when the rate was doubled. With decimalisation this was converted to ½p and was further increased to 1p as from 24th June 1974. The late fee on letters was abolished on 24th September 1976, but still remains for recorded and registered mails handed into the TPOs up to ten minutes before departure. With the introduction of the two tier mail system the service only applies to first class mail.

Late fee boxes were first introduced in 1882 and were initially hung on the sides of the carriages when they were in the station. Eventually they became part of the coach construction and are marked by a broad red band surrounding the box.

If the late fee was not paid a hand stamp 'posted without late fee' would be applied and the deficiency doubled and collected at the packet's destination.

Letters posted onto the TPOs even now receive an appropriate postmark as each TPO still carries its own hand-stamp.

Some years ago late fee posting boxes were installed at many stations throughout the country. Normally they would remain closed during the day and not be opened until a couple of hours before the departure of the TPO. They would be cleared thirty minutes before the train's departure, the contents being transferred directly to the TPO for postmarking and sorting. The rules governing the posting in these boxes was the same as for the TPOs. At the present time late posting boxes are still installed at most of London's main line stations from which TPOs leave, i.e. Paddington, King's Cross, Waterloo, Euston and Liverpool Street, as well as Exeter, Newton Abbot, Bournemouth and Newcastle.

A DIRECTORY OF INDIVIDUAL SERVICES

LONDON & EXETER T.P.O. (THE SPECIAL MAIL)

By 1854 the Post Office had decided to speed up the 'Night Mail' and at the same time forward the South Wales mails via Bristol, thus dispensing with the need for a Swindon–Gloucester mail train while introducing a sorting duty between London and Bristol, commencing on 1st February 1855. The 'Special Mail', as it was known, consisted of two sorting coaches and a van hauled by a 'Firefly' class locomotive at an average speed of 42 mph. It departed from Paddington at 8.46 p.m. with stops at Slough, Maidenhead, Reading, Steventon, Swindon, Chippenham and Bath, reaching Bristol at 12.30 a.m., where it combined with the train departing for Exeter, arriving at 3.20 a.m. and Plymouth at 5.45 a.m. The opposite working departed from Exeter at 9.45 a.m., splitting at Bristol at 12.25 a.m. and arriving at Paddington at 4.19 a.m. with the same stops on the 'up' journey as the 'down'. The combination of these two was to become the 'London & Exeter Railway Post Office' and eventually a constituent of the GW TPO.

Even though the Post Office made repeated requests for lineside apparatus, the GWR refused, believing it to be unsafe and too close to the trains. However, a new contract with the GWR and the Bristol & Exeter Railway in 1858 brought about the erection of apparatus during September that year at West Drayton, Slough, Maidenhead, Wallingford Road and Faringdon Road. They were first used by the 'Day Mail' on 1st January 1859 and by the 'Night Mail' some time in July. The coaches then in use were some of the first to be fitted with a narrow side gangway and were about 21 ft long. By 1864 additional apparatus had been erected at Southall, Twyford, Cholsey Bridge, Shrivenham and Yatton and in September 1869 at Weston Junction and Tiverton Junction.

On the 'down' service the vans were attached to the 12.40 a.m. from Bristol passenger train for forwarding to Exeter, while on the 'up' service from Bristol, the vans, having been detached from the 9.45 a.m. passenger train from Exeter, formed their own train.

A portion of the 'up' train was delayed at Plymouth on the 18th February 1860 when the train was in collision with a shunting engine, having been diverted from its own line. The van, with the mail, did not make its connection with the 'up' passenger train at Exeter, resulting in a special being run from Exeter to catch the connection at Bristol.

The 'Special Mail' title ceased in 1869 when on 14th May the Post Office agreed to an additional carriage being added to the train provided that a more powerful loco was supplied. The train became a 'Limited Mail' and such was the limit that not even the directors' passes were valid on the train without prior written authority.

In 1883 van Nos. 143-5 (L1) with only delivery arms were placed in service with Nos. 850/1 being added four years later, fitted with four traductor arms and a net apparatus. A year later in 1888 Nos. 852/3 were added as the service and the amount of mail being carried had increased.

The use of the title 'London & Exeter RPO/TPO' was to cease on 26th November 1895 with the introduction of the GW TPO, which was an amalgamation of several West of England TPOs.

THE CORNWALL SORTING TENDER

One of the other services to become part of the GW TPO was the 'Cornwall Sorting Tender'. This title actually covers two services: the 'Night Mail', which was run in connection with the 'London & Exeter RPO (Night Mail)', and a 'North Mail' which ran to meet the 'Bristol & Exeter RPO North Mail'. As the need for a sorting carriage arose, the Post Office asked the Cornwall Railway to supply a carriage for use from 1st October 1859. A coach was hired from the Bristol & Exeter Railway and a 2nd class carriage was converted with a single mail sorting compartment for secondary use. Eventually, in 1861 the Cornwall Railway provided its own van numbered 1. However, it would seem that this was still not enough to cover all the services between Exeter and Truro as there is reference to a further pair of vans being converted on 29th May 1862 at a cost of £58 each.

In 1860 the night sorting duty between Exeter and Plymouth ceased and in its place a bag tender was run through from Exeter to Plymouth to maintain the connection from the 'London & Exeter TPO'. Several years later a parcel tender was added, becoming the 'Plymouth & Exeter Night Mail Tender' which was to cease with the introduction of the 'GW TPO'.

Once the line was opened between Truro and Falmouth, the night ST ran through from Plymouth to Falmouth until 1892 when, under the GWR, trains ran through on the narrow gauge to Penzance. The service ceased as a 'Night Mail' and was combined with the 'London & Exeter RPO' on 26th November 1895 to form the 'GW TPO'. The 'North Mail' continued until 11th February 1896 when it combined with the 'Bristol & Plymouth TPO' to form the 'Bristol & Penzance TPO'.

THE WEST CORNWALL TENDER

The 'West Cornwall Tender' was the result of the break of gauge. Having taken over the Hayle Railway, a standard gauge mineral railway between Hayle and Redruth, the West Cornwall Railway extended the line to Penzance and Truro. By Act of Parliament the West Cornwall Railway had been required by the Cornwall Railway to provide broad gauge metals but in 1859 the company had no available capital to carry out this obligation. Consequently the undertaking soon became part of the Bristol & Exeter Railway and the GWR, and was managed by a joint committee until eventually passing to the GWR in 1876.

Mails were first carried between Plymouth and Truro in 1855. In 1864 a letter gives details that from 9th January 1865 bags from Penzance were to be conveyed by the 7.30 p.m. from Penzance to Truro and forwarded by a goods train departing at 10.30 p.m. If the London mail was late the return working was to wait at least 55 minutes. Carriages in use appear to have been some form of converted second class carriage and/or a converted horse-box fitted with sorting equipment, which seems to have commenced on 1st March 1884. The service was to cease with the introduction of through trains in 1892.

TRURO & FALMOUTH SORTING TENDER

Another short service was the 'Truro & Falmouth Sorting Tender'. The line from Truro was opened on 24th August 1863 and the following June a sorting duty commenced. Until 1892 the duty was an extension of the 'Cornwall Sorting Tender' (Night Mail) running through from Plymouth to Truro and Falmouth by the Cornwall Railway's van No. 1. After this it became a separate duty as the carriage ran through from Plymouth to Penzance. In 1891 the original van was relegated to standby duties, being replaced by a new 28 ft four-wheeled van No. 500. This vehicle was not fitted with apparatus, although in 1871 apparatus working had taken place at Perranwell. A second vehicle, No. 491 of 1892, was also used on the service; this was a combined luggage and sorting van. On 31st October 1896 the mail was involved in an accident to the west of Penryn station, which resulted in the loco and mail van running down a 70 ft embankment. Even with the introduction of the 'GW TPO' this service survived until 1916, when the acceleration of the 'GW TPO' eliminated the requirement for a local sorting carriage and the duty was discontinued in August 1916, although the parcels sorting had ceased on 11th December 1915.

Unfortunate incidents sometimes occurred on the TPOs and this service was to be no exception. On one occasion the officer on duty had just sealed his first bag when the seal fell to the floor and rolled into a corner under the wax pot. In stooping to pick up the seal he upset the pot and all the boiling wax, which spilled onto the back of his neck and down his collar. He did not faint, but laid there on the floor of the carriage in agony until Truro was reached some fifteen minutes later. There he was rushed to hospital and eventually made a good recovery. The mail porter at Truro stood guard over the carriage until the arrival of the 'GW TPO' some thirty minutes later, when the whole staff raced across the platform and gathered up all the ordinary and registered letters, which the unfortunate sorter had been unable to bag off, and transferred these to the 'GW TPO', which left on time without having exceeded its booked five minute stop.

GREAT WESTERN SORTING TENDER

The 'Great Western Sunday Sorting Tender' running between Paddington and Swindon commenced on 12th April 1850 but was replaced by the 'Great Western District Sorting Carriage' on 16th November 1859, running between Paddington and Exeter. This service was only to last until 24th August 1869 when it was withdrawn as an economy measure, as there was insufficient traffic for the service. Both types of services already mentioned in an earlier part of this chapter, were attempts to relieve the work loads of the TPOs.

DARTMOOR RAILWAY SORTING TENDER

A further unusual duty was the 'Dartmoor RST' which was run by the GWR at the Post Office request from Plymouth to Princetown in connection with some large scale military manoeuvres held on Dartmoor between 1st and 21st August 1873. It was never repeated for any subsequent manoeuvres.

GREAT WESTERN TRAVELLING POST OFFICE

The gauge conversion of 1892 meant that the service through to Penzance could be run on a single gauge, leading the Post Office to examine the possibility of running a number of smaller TPOs or combining them all to form one night TPO with some day TPOs of lesser importance.

On 26th November 1895 the Post Office announced that the 'Night Mail TPO' between London and Penzance would in future be called the 'Great Western Travelling Post Office'. This became the best known TPO on the GWR, partly because of the distance covered and in later years it reverted to a Special TPO once again. The service was formed from the combination of the 'London & Exeter RPO', the 'Cornwall ST' (Night Mail) and the 'Plymouth & Exeter night Mail Tender', although as previously mentioned, the 'Truro & Falmouth ST' remained until 1916, dependent entirely upon the 'GW TPO', as a separate working. It was on 1st May 1896 that the first direct sorting carriage ran through to Penzance from Paddington as part of an ordinary passenger train. Although the Post Office wished to create a 'Special' of this service, this was not sanctioned by the Treasury until October 1901.

Initially delays occurred at Plymouth through shunting as only one of the two mail vans was required to continue through to Penzance. The cause of the delays appears to have been the use of the bag tender on the Cornish section which was changed for the letter sorting carriage. To accommodate this, three Letter Sorting Carriages were fitted with apparatus in 1897 at a cost of £58 each.

With the granting of money to run a special mail train, the new 'GW TPO' began life on 1st January 1902 and comprised a 46 ft 6 ins LSC, 40 ft 3 ins Parcels Sorting Carriage, 46 ft 6 ins Bag Tenders plus various railway vans supplied by the GWR. The LSCs and BTs were all fitted with apparatus. During 1903 the TPO was reorganised to cope with the greater amount of mail being handled. New coaches were put into service but not for the complete train, an event that was not to occur until 1959.

The Sunday service was terminated at Plymouth on 12th June 1921 as no Sunday collections were then made. In later years the Sunday service was withdrawn completely. By 1934 the train in the 'up' direction was hauled on three nights a week by the same loco for the whole journey. On the 'down' journey loco changes occurred at Exeter and Newton Abbot. The 1933 loco roster is worth recording. The

Cornwall Railway TPO van No. 1 hauled by South Devon Railway 4–4–0T No. 362 *Mazeppa* on a westbound TPO in Cornwall. *Courtesy Bristol Museum*

'Atlantic' No. 183 *Red Gauntlet* at Old Oak Common on 29th October 1905 with the refurbished GW TPO, which included two new 70 ft sorting carriages. *British Railways*

rostered locomotive, a 'Castle' class from Laira shed, departed from Plymouth at 6.13 a.m. with the ex-1.40 a.m. Paddington, arriving at 8.45 a.m. at Penzance (newspaper train). Departing at 10.00 a.m. on the 'up' 'Cornish Riviera', the loco worked through to Plymouth, arriving at 12.33 p.m. The loco was serviced and returned West on the 'down' 'Cornish Riviera' (dept. 2.40 p.m.) arriving at Penzance at 5.00 p.m. After a short respite it then departed on the 'up' 'GW TPO' at 6.48 p.m. for Plymouth.

The 'GW TPO' had the most apparatus working points. These are difficult to list as they varied almost from year to year, but a selection is given in the list on page 65.

During the Second World War, the 'GWR TPO', in common with all other TPOs, was suspended from 21st September 1940 until 1st October 1945, during which period some form of bag tender service was operated. The late fee posting box was reinstated on 7th July 1947. The TPO was also suspended for a short period during the First World War between 5th November 1914 until the end of the war.

Certainly the 'GW TPO' had its fair share of incidents and particularly van No. 835 as detailed in a further volume. Fire appears to have been a great danger to the TPO, not always caused from within the TPO, as in the case of No. 851, which was lost near Bridgwater in February 1921. Smaller fires often caused minor damage as happened with No. 835 on 23rd March 1931. No. 830 was to lose a bogie spring suspension bolt at Hanwell and after inspection at Reading was to continue on to Bristol before being withdrawn from traffic. A number of minor faults in the early 1930s led to coach withdrawals, most of which are detailed under the appropriate diagram.

THE LONDON AND BRISTOL SORTING TENDER

Although combining several services, the 'GW TPO' was not the only TPO to cover the route to Penzance. Somewhat eclipsed by the 'Night Special', the daytime TPOs were to fill an important part of the services. The first of these, the 'London & Bristol Sorting Tender', commenced in 1841 as far as Bristol, but was extended to Exeter in 1844 as a bag tender. Sorting commenced on 1st April 1868 from Paddington to Bristol only, at which time the carriage was attached to a different train at Bristol for forwarding to Exeter.

On 1st June 1875, the GWR introduced an early morning parcels train from Paddington, departing at 5.30 a.m. The Post Office took the opportunity to attach the sorting coach to this train rather than the later departure of 9.00 a.m. The main use of this service was the transfer of mails which had arrived in London on the early TPOs, or failed to connect with the previous night's TPOs, onwards to the west.

Stock used was usually one of the combined passenger/sorting coaches of 1889, No. 2085 being allocated for a period. The 'up' duty ceased during the First World War from 13th October 1917 and was not resumed until 6th June 1932, when it was retimed as a result of the later departures of the TPOs from London, and also renamed the 'Bristol–London TPO'.

Apparatus was in use in 1930 at Hayes, West Drayton, Slough and Maidenhead, but only at the latter two the following year. The service, like others, was suspended for the Second World War on 21st September 1940 and never restored.

With the retiming of the 'London & Bristol Sorting Tender' in 1875, a TPO was still required between Bristol and Exeter on the 9.00 a.m. departure from Paddington, viz. the 'Bristol & Exeter TPO (Day)'. By 1893 it appears that the carriage returned empty from Exeter, while a year later the service received a new carriage fitted with apparatus. The coach was fully converted to a TPO in the early 1900s, lasting until the service ceased in 1917.

THE PLYMOUTH–BRISTOL TPO

The 'Plymouth–Bristol TPO' commenced on 1st December 1859 as the 'Bristol & Exeter RPO (North Mail)'. However, this was not the same as the 'North Mail' which formed the forerunner to the 'GW TPO' since this service connected with the 'Midland TPO' at Bristol. The service was intended to cut the long delay at Bristol between the arrival and departure of the mail from the north and that from Exeter. Initially as an experiment, the use of an existing second class compartment with fittings for sorting was tried, but in 1861 a sorting carriage was evidently in use, as on 4th November the Post Office requested the fitting of side lights to the vehicle. In February 1863 there was a further request to move the carriage to the centre of the train as there seems to have been some poor riding qualities to the coach concerned. By 12th September 1866, the Sunday service had ceased.

Early in July 1872 the duty was extended to Newton Abbot and renamed the 'Bristol & Newton Abbot TPO' between 1873 and 1875. With the acceleration of the West of England and South Wales mail services in 1892, the service was further extended to Plymouth and further renamed the 'Bristol & Plymouth TPO' on 15th October 1895. Timings were such as to connect with the 'Cornwall ST (North Mail)' 'up' and 'down', with the result that in the 'up' direction the connection with the 'Midlands TPO' was lost at Bristol, (a connection not remade until 1922) but gained with the 'Bristol, Shrewsbury & Normanton TPO'. On 11th February 1896 the 'Bristol–Plymouth TPO' and the 'Cornwall ST (North Mail)' were abolished and the coaches run through to Penzance to form the 'Bristol & Penzance TPO'.

In 1896 coaches No. 2080, 2084 and 2086 were in use, partially fitted with passenger accommodation. This was removed at the request of the Post Office and fitted for parcels sorting. Corridor connectors were also fitted allowing access to other postal vehicles.

On 14th August 1916 the Post Office, as part of the war economy, reduced the 'North Mail' to Bristol–Plymouth only, a reduction that was to remain even though the coach ran through to Penzance in the train empty until 1924, but not until 26th March 1930 did the service become known as the 'Bristol–Plymouth TPO' or 'Plymouth–Bristol TPO' dependent on the direction.

1933 had seen the introduction of two new carriages on this service, Nos. 799 and 800, the latter being the spare held at Bristol. Both coaches were equipped with electric radiators for use while standing at Bristol. The service used apparatus and in 1914 was worked at St. Germans, Liskeard, Lostwithiel, St. Austell, Grampound Road, Scorrier, Redruth, Cambourne and Marazion, but by 1958 this had been reduced to only two locations.

Suspended between the 21st September 1940 and 21st May 1948, for the duration of the Second World War, the service was slowly reduced until withdrawn on 3rd March 1972, its greatest use having been in the 'down' direction.

BRISTOL & DERBY TPO

Although not a GWR train, this TPO is included briefly to complete the northwards picture. The 'Bristol & Derby TPO' began life as a Bag Tender from Bristol to Gloucester in 1899, connecting with the 'GW TPO' 'up' and 'down' at Bristol. A sorting duty commenced on 1st June 1910 under the title of the 'Gloucester & Bristol TPO (Night)'. The 1915 roster shows Midland coaches in use on the service. On 13th July 1925 the 'South Wales TPO' was altered from Gloucester to Bristol, so making a connection with this TPO. The duty was extended to Birmingham on 3rd July 1938 and, after suspension for the Second World War, was further extended to Derby in March 1949 due to platform difficulties at Birmingham.

SOUTH WALES TPO (NORTH MAIL)

South Wales was not without its TPO services, having a 'North Mail' and a 'Night Mail' running east/west through the industrial area. To connect with the north, two outlets were to be available in the form of a connection at Bristol with the 'Bristol–Derby TPO' and at Cardiff with a north bound TPO via Shrewsbury. The wilder west coast of Wales too was connected to Shrewsbury with a TPO from Aberystwyth.

The origins of the TPOs in South Wales date back to 1850 when from 25th July the South

An interior view of TPO coach No. 838 allocated to the Bristol-Penzance TPO. This photo was taken at Penzance on 9th January 1900 prior to the majority of mail arriving for the return trip. The sorter furthest from the camera is sorting in the registered packet frame. *British Railways*

Wales line was in use from Chepstow to Swansea with the mails travelling on the 4.25 a.m. from Chepstow and the 5.15 p.m. from Swansea. These mail trains were virtually specials, as far as the railway company was concerned. The discontinuance of the mail coach via Gloucester and its substitution of a mail leaving Bristol at 1.30 a.m., crossing the River Severn at 3.00 a.m. in an open boat, precluded any passenger traffic on the 'down' service, while the 'up' service was little better with a passenger traffic receipt of 2/4d per mile. The situation was not improved when on 11th November 1851 the train timings were advanced by one hour in both directions. The line between Gloucester and Chepstow had been opened on 19th September 1851, but with the bridge across the Wye still to be completed, it was 19th July 1852 before the through route could be opened.

The first mention of the 'North Mail' appears in 1852 although it was not until 1st March 1884 that any sorting was carried out on the service, when the 'South Wales TPO (North Mail)' commenced running from Gloucester (where connection was made with the 'Midland TPO') to New Milford (Neyland), the point of arrival and departure of the southern Irish ferries. The service ran on weekdays only and catered for both letter and parcel sorting. The 1895 roster had two 27 ft coaches of 1872 in use with a spare on standby. All were gas lit and equipped with apparatus.

The 1915 roster had two 40 ft coaches of 1892 in use. Until 8th March 1904 the service had officially been classed as a Sorting Carriage but from this date it became a TPO. From 6th November 1916 the service was reduced from New Milford to Swansea only, with no apparatus workings along the route, an operation which had required the turning of the coaches. With the development of the TPO services, the 'North Mail' was withdrawn on 29th October 1923, having run its last trip on the 27th.

THE SOUTH WALES TPO (NIGHT MAIL)

The establishment of a 'Night Mail' was to improve the circulation of mail in the area in connection with the main night mails in the rest of the country. Bag Tenders were running prior to 1860 and apparatus working was introduced three years later at Briton Ferry and in 1864 at Kidwelly and St. Clears. It was not until 1st March 1869 that the full service of a TPO commenced between Gloucester and New Milford as a 'Night Mail', with a coach running through as a Bag Tender to Swindon from Gloucester to connect with the London night mails service.

The 'South Wales TPO (Night Mail)' was soon in trouble when an accident between Swindon and Gloucester on 11th March 1869 required the re-routeing of the service for a short period. Parcels sorting commenced in November 1885 with an extra coach for this purpose being added in December 1891, initially between Gloucester and Swansea but extended to New Milford in January 1892. During 1892 two new coaches, Nos. 860 and 861L, were allocated to the service, each fitted with apparatus.

By 1924 the service terminated at Carmarthen and, with the acceleration of the 'GW TPO', the eastern terminus was moved from Gloucester to Bristol on 13th July 1925. The connection with the 'Bristol–Derby TPO' at Gloucester was subsequently made at Bristol. A Bag Tender was still run through from London to Neyland in 1928, forming part of the 'South Wales TPO' between Bristol and Carmarthen.

In common with most other TPOs, this service received new coaches in the 1932 period but they were not equipped with apparatus, the working of which having ceased in 1930.

Suspended on 21st September 1940 for the Second World War, the service was reinstated on 6th May 1946 when the western terminus reverted to New Milford until February 1969, when once again it was changed to Carmarthen.

CAMARTHEN & NEWCASTLE EMLYN SORTING COACH

Carmarthen was also the terminus of another service, the 'Carmarthen & Newcastle Emlyn SC', which was established on 14th December 1875 between Carmarthan and Llandyssul as

Post Office staff posed by the 1887 built stowage van No. 850. This vehicle formed part of the GW TPO at the turn of the century. *Post Office*

a 'Night Mail' in both directions and as a 'Day Mail' to Llandyssul only, the tender returning empty to operate the Day (North) Mail service. Both services were timed to connect with the South Wales TPOs.

In 1891 the Post Office asked the GWR for newer coaches with increased space for sorting and larger doors. As requested, two coaches were supplied later that year. They were four-wheeled 28 ft vans without apparatus or corridor connections. With the extension of the line the service was extended to Newcastle Emlyn in 1895, but it ceased completely on 1st May 1904 when the coaches were returned to the GWR as Parcel Brake Vans.

CARDIFF–CREWE TPO

The present day 'Cardiff–Crewe TPO' has its origin in the 'Shrewsbury & Crewe SC' first established on 1st April 1891. This service was amalgamated with the 'Normanton & Stalybridge TPO' on 1st February 1893, to become the 'Shrewsbury & Normanton TPO' which was replaced by the 'Bristol, Shrewsbury & Normanton TPO' on 6th November 1895. In turn this service became the 'Bristol, Shrewsbury & York TPO' on 1st July 1902, becoming the 'Cardiff & York (Night Mail) TPO' on 7th June 1910. This lasted until 5th October 1920 when it was divided to form the 'Shrewsbury & York Railway Sorting Carriage' and the 'Cardiff–Crewe Railway Sorting Carriage'. The title was changed to that of a TPO on 25th June 1934.

It is interesting to note that the arrangements arrived at in 1920 are still in use today. The sorting carriage was attached to the 1.55 a.m. train from Crewe instead of the later 1.40 a.m. where connection had been made with the 'down' and 'up' 'Special TPO' and the 'NW TPO' night 'down'. There were no stops at Hereford or Abergavenny although apparatus was worked at the latter. Three 1892 carriages, Nos. 862, 864 and 865, were allotted to the service, each of which was equipped with letter and parcel sorting frames. No. 864 was removed from traffic when a buffer fell off between Cardiff and Newport while working this service. In 1933 these coaches were replaced by three new 50 ft vehicles, Nos. 801, 802 and 803. They were fitted with electric radiators for standing at Crewe but no apparatus, the working of which ceased by 1933 with the introduction of these vehicles. A note appears in the roster books from this date that no coach with any apparatus including traductor arms, brackets or sweep plates was to be allowed on this route.

The TPO was suspended for the Second World War from 21st September 1940 until 7th October 1946. The GWR coaches were replaced by BR coaches but the service continued as before.

ABERYSTWYTH–SHREWSBURY SORTING COACH

From Shrewsbury a further cross-country TPO ran to Aberystwyth. The 'Aberystwyth–Shrewsbury SC' has its origins in the carriage of mails by the Cambrian Railways from Shrewsbury to Borth from 1st January 1864 on passenger trains. The following year an agreement was signed with the LNWR for that company to operate the service with their coaching stock, commencing from 1st January 1865. (Table 15). The designation of Sorting

Sorting the South Devon mails in No. 806 on the GW TPO on the night of 1st July 1935.
Post Office

Carriage does not appear to have taken effect until 1883, possibly from 17th October. The Cambrian soon supplied their own TPO coach, No. 200, in 1888, replacing the 22 ft 6 ins LNWR coach No. 4 of 1860 which had been in use on the service for a number of years. This vehicle was later to be replaced by another Cambrian coach, No. 293, which was to become GWR No. 811. This was one of the TPOs suspended for a period towards the end of the First World War from 2nd June 1917, although parcels sorting had ceased earlier on 13th May 1916, to 1st July 1919, from which time the service also ran on Sundays. The title was changed to the 'Shrewsbury–Aberystwyth SC' on 8th September 1930, but the service was withdrawn on 22nd September 1939 and not reinstated.

When the GWR took over the Cambrian Railways and the responsibility for the TPO service, the early Cambrian coach was condemned on sight. The more modern coach of 1902 was in far better condition and was one of the few to be transferred to the GW stock list, re-diagrammed and renumbered into the GW series. The coach remained on the service until replaced by a GWR coach when it was transferred to the spare coach list. No. 811 was replaced in 1926 by No. 863, becoming the spare, but with the general replacement of stock in the 1930s No. 811 was soon condemned. No. 863 was replaced by 797 with 796 as spare.

CAMBRIAN FEEDER SERVICES

The Cambrian Railways also operated a number of feeder services connecting with the main Sorting Carriage. They were not TPOs but services over which the Postmaster General had control. A few months after the agreement between the Cambrian and the LNWR to operate its service in 1865, a mail contract was given to the Mid Wales Railway to carry the mails from Brecon to connect with the SC at Caersws Junction, later to be known as Moat Lane Junction. Initially, the service ran to Llanidloes and commenced on 1st January 1865, but was extended through to Brecon from 1st May. It is not clear from the original documents exactly whose stock was used, but the service formed part of the contract with the LNWR signed on 1st January 1865. It seems possible that in later years, after being displaced from the main SC, coach No. 200 was employed on this service before being condemned.

A further controlled service was Cemmaes Road to Dinas Mawddwy on the Mawddwy Railway. An inventory taken of the stock on 12th June 1909 lists one 'Kalamazoo car' in the loco shed, noted as being manually powered and for the carriage of mails. Following the cessation of passenger services on 8th April 1908, the mails were manually operated on a trolley by Mr. Abiah Williams, a fireman, working over the whole length of the line on each weekday morning and evening. Arrangements were made with Mr. John Humphries of Cemmaes Road to take over the mail contract from Dinas Mawddwy, from 1st January 1910, using his pony and van.

The Cambrian's logical desire to handle the mails for most of west Wales led to their successful bid against the GWR for the carriage of the mails from Dolgelley, via Penmaenpool. The contract commenced on 1st January 1868 although the branch was not open through to Dolgelley until 21st June 1869. In later years the GWR were to convert a single V16 coach for the use of the Dolgelley Branch mails and build two TPO vans for the same service, indicating that the GWR probably took over the mail contract from the Cambrian in 1877.

Brunel instigated a scheme for the GWR to build a line across central Wales from Worcester, via Ludlow, Craven Arms, Montgomery, Newtown & Dolgelley to the proposed harbour at Porth Dinlleyn on the north coast of the Lleyn Peninsula. This was to be the port for the cross-channel ferries to Ireland, but the scheme was doomed to failure on the completion of George Stephenson's survey of a coast line to Holyhead from Chester.

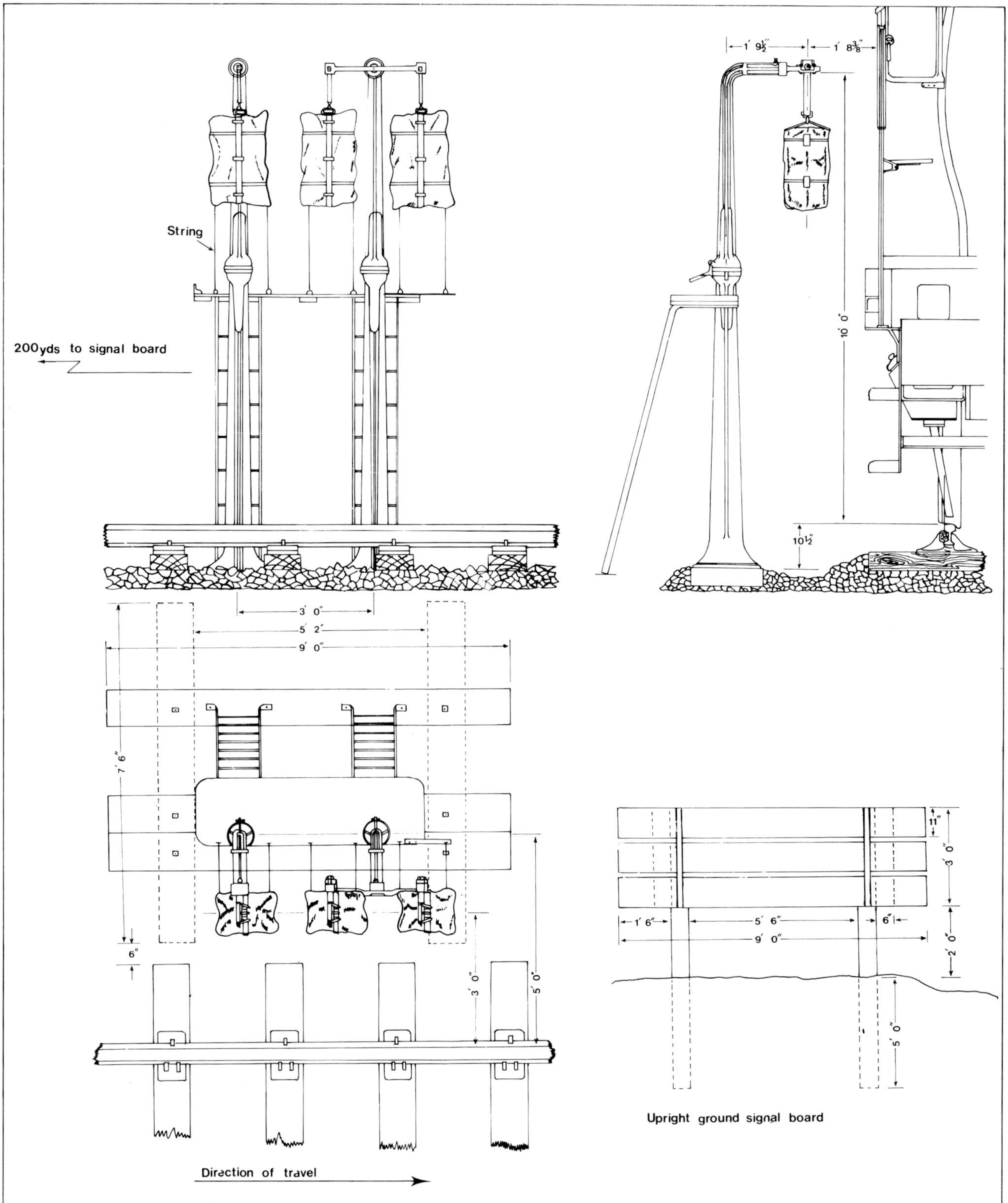

WAYSIDE PICK-UP APPARATUS

CHAPTER TWO

THE EXCHANGE APPARATUS

AFTER watching the TPO exchange apparatus in use in March 1853, Brunel and the directors of the Great Western Railway believed that the operation was full of dangers. However, prior to its introduction, the exchange of mail bags had still taken place without the train stopping, the mail guard throwing bags out of his van onto the platform and catching the bags offered to him from the ground at the end of a long pole! This somewhat amazing operation predictably resulted in a number of injuries and accidents. The GWR in particular were requested by the Post Office to slow down, especially at West Drayton where in June and December 1840 the mail guard received injuries to his hands in the course of the exchanges.

The development of the exchange apparatus was a logical progression in the process of speeding up the mails, avoiding the need to stop at many of the minor stations. The first travelling post office apparatus was built by Nathaniel Worsdell, Superintendent of coach building for the Grand Junction Railway, whose father had built the tender for Stephenson's *Rocket.* He took out a patent on 4th January 1838 which he offered to the Post Office for £3,500. When the Post Office responded with an offer of only £500 he reduced his asking price to £1,500, and later withdrew the patent offer with the intention of granting a licence to the railway companies to use the apparatus at the rate of £1 per mile per year. From the Grand Junction Railway alone this would have earned an income of £200 per annum.

The Post Office decided to produce their own apparatus, designed by John Ramsey, a senior clerk in the Post Office Secretary's office. His first experiments at Boxmoor, Hemel Hempstead on 30th May 1838, were followed by the instruction to erect further equipment at Berkhampstead and Leighton Buzzard on 14th June and Watford and Blisworth on 20th June 1838. The parts were made by Messrs. Barrow and Turner of 38 East Street, Manchester Square, London, and were erected at the locations in October of that year for further experiments which commenced on 27th of that month.

John Dicker, who had been appointed as Inspector of Mail Coaches in October 1839, simplified and improved Ramsey's apparatus at his own expense, conducting trials at Croydon in April 1848 with a coach fitted with a net and using leather exchange pouches. These were supplied at a cost of 24/- for small envelopes, 26/- for the small pouch and 30/- for the larger by

Although this photograph is not of the GWR it is ideal to illustrate the Post Office's complete wayside apparatus ready for an approaching TPO on 12th June 1907. The coach personnel had to know the exact locations of the equipment and bridges or other obstructions either side of it. This apparatus point was placed shortly after a tunnel near Watford. *Post Office*

a Mr. Hayward of Hosier Lane, Smithfield, London. The arms projecting from the coach were first termed 'traductors' by John Dicker at the time of these experiments. His apparatus was a success with only one failure in six months. If used, Dicker's apparatus would have infringed Worsdell's patent so the situation was left until the expiration of Worsdell's patent, and on 4th January 1852 Dicker's apparatus was brought into use.

The parts for the new apparatus were manufactured by William Rutler of 25 Gopsall Street, Birmingham and the basic design was to remain virtually unchanged throughout its life. One change made was to the colour of the signal lamp used, from blue light to a white as there had been some difficulty in seeing the blue. Further improvements followed a report on the system by Sir William Cubitt that the maximum weight of the pouches should be fixed at 70 lbs and a minimum of 40 lbs, although these recommendations were only adopted for a time.

Despite their mail contract the GWR refused to allow any form of apparatus working to take place on the system, hence the injuries to the mail guard at West Drayton in 1840. When Brunel was invited to view the apparatus in operation in March 1853, he admitted that the apparatus was exceedingly well devised for the particular circumstances under which he saw it work, but he could not possibly recommend it to the Board of the GWR. Its application to GWR carriages was not possible as projections of twenty inches or more could not be accommodated within the clearances of the broad gauge which already made maximum use of the available space. He also felt that the speed of GWR express trains of 30 yards a second would add to the dangers of the operation of the apparatus. The directors concurred fearing the serious accidents which might occur. However, the 1858 General Mail Contract between the Post Office, the GWR and the Bristol & Exeter Railway stipulated the provision of exchange apparatus at five locations, West Drayton, Slough, Maidenhead, Wallingford Road and Faringdon Road. It was brought into use on 1st January 1859 and assisted with acceleration of the West of England mails. The GWR's concern was not entirely unfounded as on 6th October 1862 an accident occurred at Slough in which considerable damage was caused to the locomotive and the train when the wooden supports to the ground net gave way due to rot.

On 17th September 1862, without informing his employers, John Dicker took out a patent for various modifications to the apparatus. They were tried out at Watford on 15th September 1864, and put into service at Cholsey bridge in October 1865. His demands for payment from the Post Office, which he had since left, were treated with little sympathy until 1870 when he finally received a payment of £500.

During the 1870s the number of apparatus points continued to expand, with the 978 daily exchanges in 1875 increasing to 1090 the following year. The largest number of failures was caused by the fracture of the ground standards which in 1881 amounted to 90.

Between 1860 and 1870 a number of different mechanical arms were tried, but none were as satisfactory as the standard one then in use and in June 1869 a sugges-

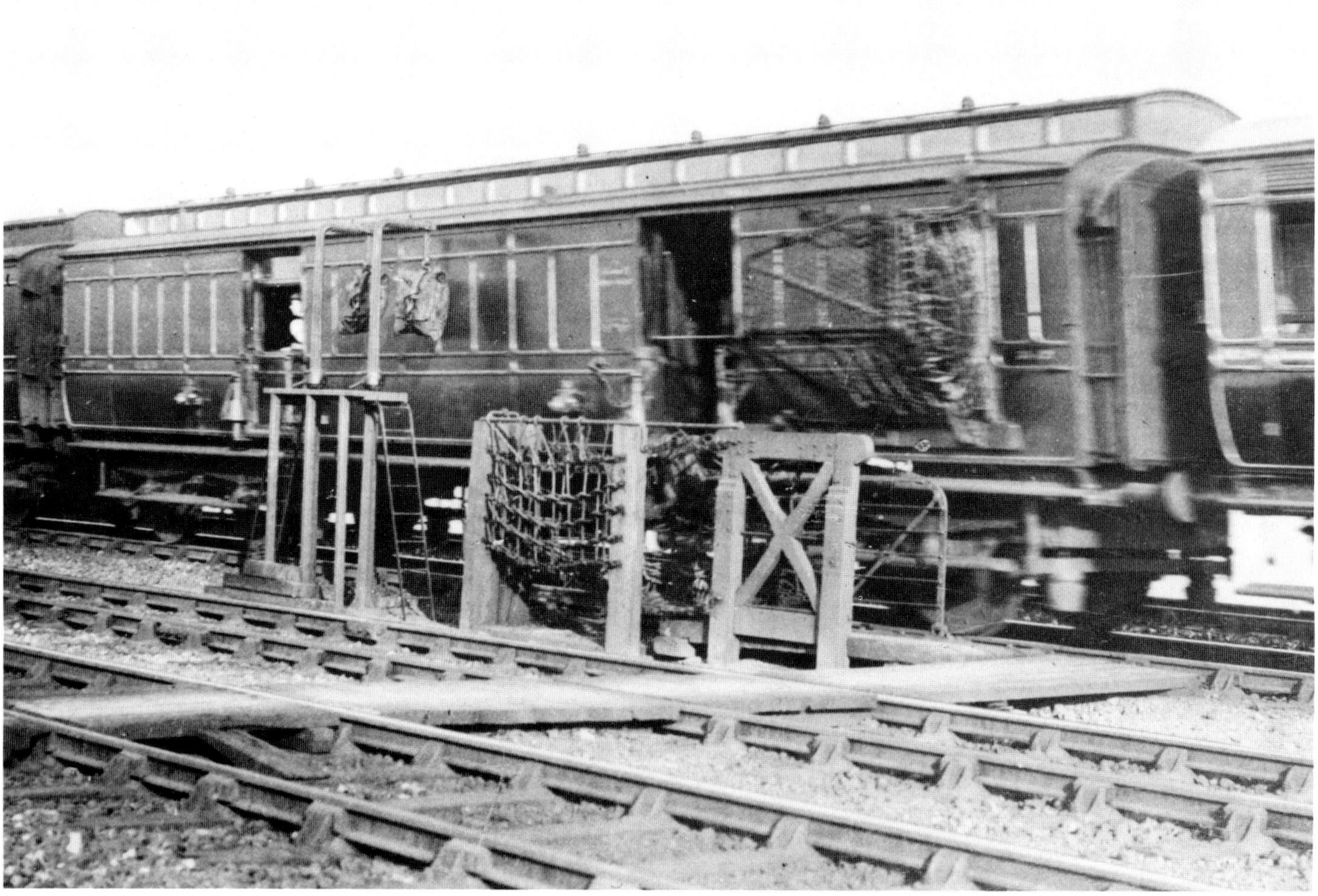

One out and two in as the TPO speeds past one of the GWR apparatus points, possibly the original Swindon location. The returning traductor arms can just be seen.
Author's collection

A close-up view of the exchange apparatus on coach No. 853 of 1905 (Diagram L15). This picture was taken in October 1925 following underframe repairs and clearly shows the two traductor arms either side of the doorway with the safety bar in its normal position. The detaching rope for receiving the ground pouches can just be seen inside the extended coach net. The spiked board for hanging post office bags would not normally be in place if the apparatus was in use. Below the GR crest is the holder for the late fee box which was hung outside the coach at stations. These were removed during travel and stored inside the coach. *British Railways*

tion by Arthur Swan, Examiner of Bag Apparatus, to increase the weight of pouches for delivery to 150 lbs, was made but was not proceeded with.

Improvements to the carriage apparatus were tested at Shrivenham in 1884 and placed in service on the 'South Wales Night TPO' on 21st July 1885. Although tested to 76 mph at Shrivenham, the improvements were not so successful in traffic and so Mr. Garrett replaced Swan's trigger catch with his own 'pin cap box'. The ground stands were also altered to give a clearance of 18 inches rather than the previous ten inches when used with the net. This reduced the number of standards being fractured but did not completely solve the problem. Although the apparatus had remained basically in its original form, the final type of pin box was not introduced until January 1900. It was designed by Mr. Bussell, Supervisor of Bag Apparatus.

The final improvement of any significance was the lengthening of the arms carried out in April 1904 by Mr. Halfpenny, following complaints from the traders at Weston-Super-Mare who were receiving a large number of damaged packets.

A number of improvements were, however, made to the apparatus as a direct result of various accidents, the first of which concerned George Simmonds who, in September 1858, had been knocked off his apparatus and killed. Following this a ladder was placed against the standards which the postman had previously climbed. The staging was further added to following another mishap to the Post Master at Cranlington in January 1884 when he slipped and fell on his back on the running line. The pouches were originally hung fifteen minutes before the booked time of the mail train but, following an incident at Newnham, gongs were installed in the apparatus huts connected to the local signal box or station.

The mere presence of the lineside equipment presented a hazard through no fault of its own. On 13th February 1880 a fireman taking the rake from the tender was swept off his engine when the end of the implement came into contact with the apparatus standards. Miraculously he was not too much the worse for his experience and was able to climb back onto the engine.

A more serious accident involved the 'down' 'Bristol & Exeter Day Mail' on 4th March 1880. Two incidents occurred, both caused by the same person and both due to the net being left extended after the apparatus point. At Weston Junction telegraph wires were brought down with no damage to the net or the train. However, at Wellington, it was quite a different story. The net was again left out following the apparatus point and demolished a signal and part of the somewhat solidly built goods shed before it was torn off with part of the coach side. One man in the goods shed was killed although the report does not indicate how this happened. Subsequently net alarms were fitted to the carriages to prevent a similar occurrence.

The first passenger to be killed by a suspended pouch was a young woman named Pirie on 19th February 1889. She was leaning out of the carriage droplight on the approach to the apparatus point when her head came into contact with a suspended pouch of 50 lbs; Pirie died a few hours later from injuries received. Following this accident the instruction was given that where apparatus working occurred on a service train, the mail coach was to travel next to the locomotive, or at least ahead of the passenger coaches. To the same effect GWR coaches of diagram L3 had horizontal guard bars fitted across the droplight windows on the net apparatus side.

The first large sliding doors were fitted to mail coaches in 1865 along with the horizontal safety bar across the aperture space, the latter having first appeared in 1860 with the double inward opening doors. These bars were fitted in an attempt to stop personnel falling out of the carriages while operating the traductor arms. They went out of use in the 1870s

Again not Great Western but an ideal view to show a pouch being lowered away on the traductor arm, an operation usually carried out at speed (often on cold wet nights!) with only the safety bar to prevent the postman from falling out. The coach, a West Coast Joint Stock vehicle, was not at the time fitted with a receiving net, although its base plate can be seen in position. *Post Office*

No. 2085 attached to the 5.30 a.m. from Paddington as the London and Bristol Sorting Carriage at Didcot in 1892 or 1893. The Post Office staff have lowered the net and arms for the photographer on a summer morning while the loco takes water. *Author's collection*

but were reinstated after an accident at 6.00 a.m. to the 'down' 'London & Bristol SC' on 5th December 1897. At this time six pouches were exchanged at Slough but the coach in use had only four arms. The method employed was for four bags to be despatched prior to the station and the remaining two after. While loading the arms for the second drop, the sorter, Albert Latchford, lost his balance and fell out of the carriage. He was killed instantly from a fractured skull. The safety bars were reinstated on all coaches the following year and remained in use till the end of apparatus working.

Mention has already been made of the standards fracturing and the improvements made. In September and November 1899 two standards fractured at Hitchin and Yatton with the broken sections falling through the windows of the following carriages. Both were due to a flaw in the casting, but fortunately no one was injured even though both compartments were occupied at the time.

The problem of when to drop the traductor arms and net from the coach was often the cause of accidents. The apparatus operators were always well versed in the location of various features along the line, such as bridges and signals, but mistakes did occur. On 19th September 1900 the apparatus was put out at the wrong place on the 'South Wales SC'. A bridge at Awre was mistaken for one prior to Newnham resulting in the net being smashed with considerable damage to the carriage.

A more amusing incident occurred at St. Austell where the apparatus mark was on a steep bank some distance from the station. Because of the speed restriction there it was not unusual for the Grampound Road to St. Austell bag to be left out of the pouch and thrown onto the platform as the train passed slowly through. On this occasion, however, a rather heavy bag was discovered as the apparatus was approached and since it was too late to put it in the pouch, the officer decided to cover his error by dropping it on the station. To make this easier he rather foolishly removed the safety bar from the door and as the train was travelling faster than usual he fell out with the bag! The communication cord was pulled and the rest of the staff rushed back to be met by the unfortunate man running for all he was worth after the train. He had landed on top of the bag which had contained newspapers and was only bruised and shaken. Rule 10 of the Rules and Regulations of Officers of TPOs states: 'Having taken up duty, Officers are not to leave the mail without sanction of their Officer in charge.' When he returned to the carriage the overseer handed him a form P18 instructing him to account why he had left the train without permission!

The ground or wayside apparatus consisted of two parts, receiving and despatching, the actual layout being tailored to the local conditions. In general the wayside collection net was placed ahead of the despatching standards of which there could be up to 4 sets. The location of the apparatus point would be such that there would be no obstructions within 4 ft 9 ins of the track for 250 yards preceding the point and none for 300 yards following. Once erected, the location of the apparatus had to be known exactly by the apparatus officer on the TPO, a description being kept up to date in the 'Marks' book which was kept aboard the TPO. Warning boards, placed some 200 to 250 yards ahead of the point, took the form of one of two types, either that shown in the drawing or a 24 ft long white painted board laid alongside the track on the ground in such a position that it could be seen from the coach. A further warning board associated with the ground apparatus was the yellow and black chequered enamelled sign placed on the approach side of the apparatus, often on the rear of the hut. This was to warn the locomotive crew of the position of the apparatus and was illuminated at night when the apparatus was to be used. In common with the lights on the side of the coaches, the lamps would be used from thirty minutes before sunset until thirty minutes after sunrise. At the pre-determined point known exactly by the TPO crew, the apparatus would be lowered out in readiness for the exchange which was over in seconds as the train sped by, the apparatus being returned to its stowage position clear of any lineside obstructions. The exact positioning of the apparatus was important in relation to the carriage, even allowing for any swaying of the train and the loading of the carriages. All the dimensions quoted and on the drawings relating to the apparatus on page 12 are for the GWR and British Railways Western Region, who required a larger clearance to allow for stock built to the full proportions of the gauge, such as the Dreadnought coaches.

Occasionally the apparatus had to be set up between running lines as in this case. Again this is believed to be the original Swindon location. *Author's collection*

Prior to departure of the TPO, the carriage apparatus was tested, often in the station when sorters arrived for the duty. The lighting and heating, along with the emergency systems for both, were also tested and the failure of either of these systems could cause the withdrawal of a vehicle from the service.

Mail bags were despatched from the coach on spring-loaded 'traductor arms' attached to either side of the large sliding doors along the coach side. Most later GWR coaches had a width over panels, at at the waist of 8 ft 6 ins. This could effectively be increased to as much as 9 ft 10 ins with all the projections of the apparatus. The bags would be suspended, on the traductor arm, 3 ft out from the coach side with the pin box being 4 ft 8¼ ins above the rail. The pouch was suspended by a leather strap which had to be capable of withstanding the impact when it came into contact with the wire or steel bar support across the entrance to the ground net. Once separated, the traductor arm would return to its out of use position when it was sprung vertically against the side of the coach. If the spring failed a rope was provided for pulling the

Left: Seconds before this outgoing pouch is snatched by the ground net. *Right:* The moment of exchange caught on film. Two pouches are snatched from the coach and the traductor arms can be seen returning to the coach side, while a single pouch awaits to be whisked away. This shot comes from a film made to establish exactly what happened during the exchange in the hope of finding improvements to the system. *Post Office*

WAYSIDE COLLECTION APPARATUS

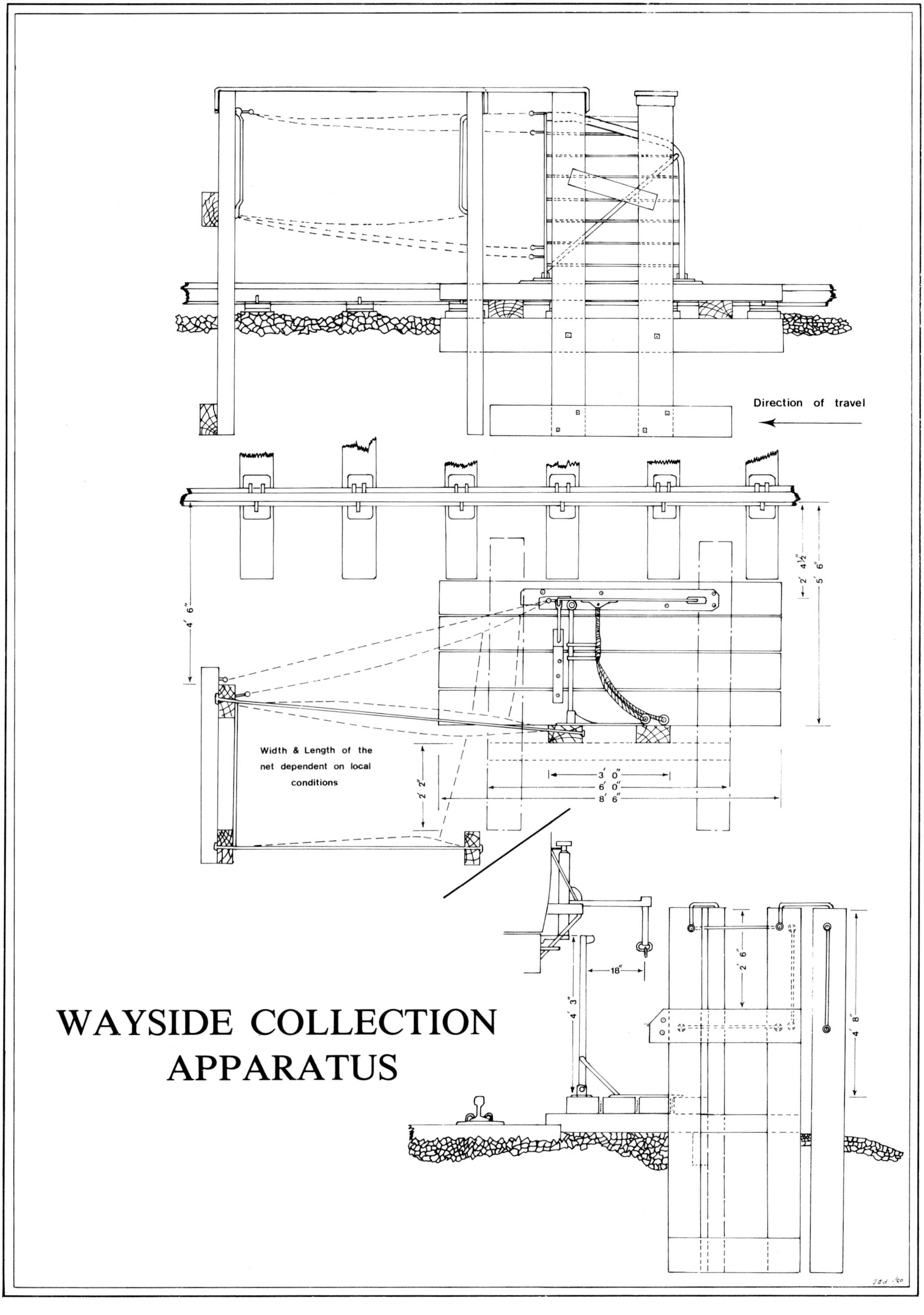

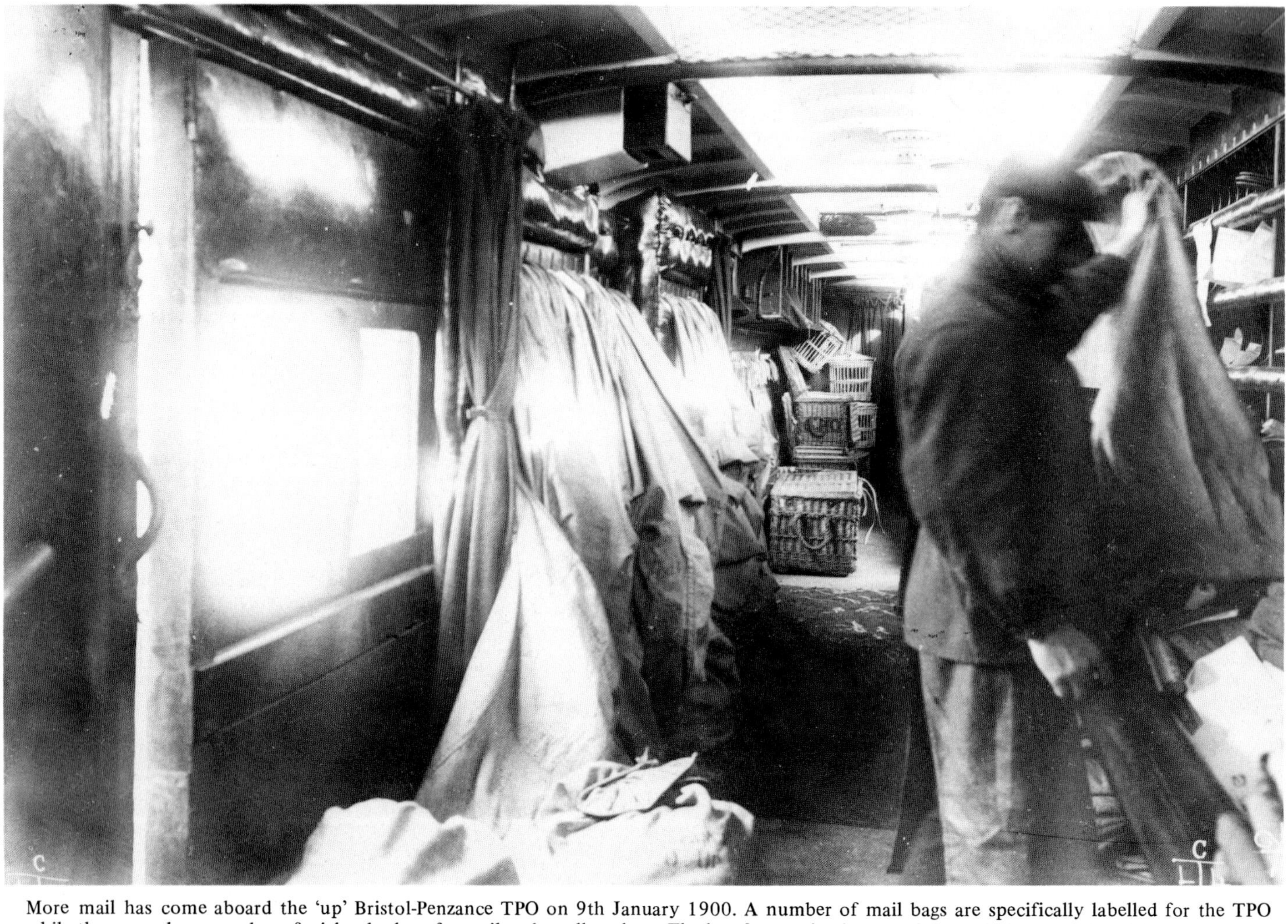

More mail has come aboard the 'up' Bristol-Penzance TPO on 9th January 1900. A number of mail bags are specifically labelled for the TPO while there are also a number of wicker baskets for mail and small packets. The late fee posting box can be seen in its stowed position in the roof.
British Railways

arm to the stowage position where it could be tied in out of use.

The wayside net was designed to detach the bag from the traductor arm and then catch it, stopping the forward momentum of the bag within a few feet. The size of the net was dependent upon the requirement of mails to be exchanged and the available space at each site. The roped part of the net was set away from the lineside slightly and reinforced with chains suspended from sleepers set into the ground, the latter being sunk to a sufficient depth not to collapse with continuous heavy use. The postman on the ground recovered the bags from behind the net, a standing instruction forbidding the postman from passing on the line side of it. The side frame of the net support when set ready for use was only 2 ft 4½ ins from the line side, so it was folded away from the line to give greater clearance when out of use.

Pouches for collection were suspended from the standards by similar leather straps and hung from a pin box identical to those used on the carriage traductor arms. The standards were 10 ft tall with the top section being made to swivel round and away from the track when not in use. Normally there would be two standards at one point, one of which, by virtue of an extension bar, was able to hold two bags. This would always be the second of the standards. Ladders and a small platform were provided so that the postman could reach the standard tops to attach the pouches to the pin box. Normally the ladders were situated to the rear of the standards but, according to the location, the ladder could be placed to one side of the standards. The pouches were attached about ten minutes before the train was due and after the signal from the local signal box that the TPO was expected the postman would swivel the standards into position and erect the net. There was a clearance of only 1 ft 8 ins between the locomotive cab side and the pin box and this was further reduced by about 5 ins by the pouch. The pouches were tied to the wooden platform to hold them steady in the passing rush of air from the train. The cord used was critical as tarred cord or sisal twist would not break as required and was liable to damage the leather bags.

The coach net would be extended at the same point at which the traductor arms were lowered. The net was operated by a long counter-balanced lever in the coach and was lowered after the net door had been opened. The lever was not attached to the net frame but bore against it in such a way that if it failed or became damaged the net could be recovered by hand. A special stop would then have to be made to inspect the net and if necessary to detach the coach from the train. Once the net was lowered, a bell would sound continuously inside the coach, warning of the forthcoming exchange. The six inch bell was mounted in the locked 'weights recess' space so no unauthorised persons could interfere with its operation. It was powered by three Leclanché cells and operated by a contact mounted on the exterior of the coach. As the net was lowered, a steel pin rotated the external contact arm through 45°, making the circuit within the contact box. Apart from warning staff of the exchange and not to pass by the net door, it also warned that the net was extended. Wooden barriers were also placed across the corridor doors to stop the staff passing into the area where the bags came flying in, as in many vehicles this area would be close to the corridor connection door. The net, extending 2 ft 4 ins from the side of the coach, also had a detaching wire at a height that would come into contact with the vertical leather strap of the pouch. In the same style as the wayside net, the pouch would be detached from the standard with some force and tumble into the coach from the net. The rear of the carriage net was reinforced with additional rope as bags would be whisked from rest to the speed of the train in the length of the net. Rope was used in preference to any other material as it would not damage the leather pouches and their contents.

Once the apparatus point was passed, the net was returned to its stowage position and the interior lever locked in the upright position. The large doors had to be open for the whole operation and, although this was over in seconds, the need to shut the doors as soon as possible, particularly on a cold, damp and windy night, is easily imagined. This must have been even more important in dual purpose coaches where the exchange and sorting were carried out in the same

Fixing a pouch to a wayside standard. *Post Office*

Operating the coach net lever in a GWR vehicle. *Post Office*

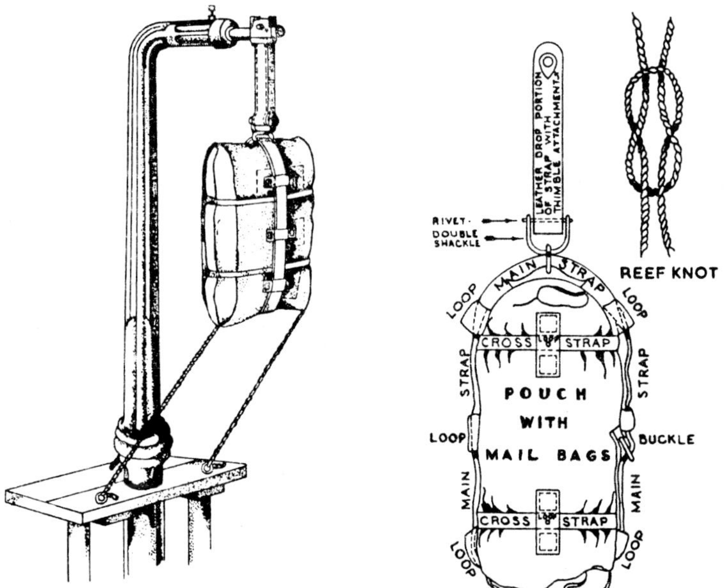

METHOD OF SUSPENDING & TYING IN POUCH TO STANDARD PLATFORM

vehicle! Heavy green felt curtains were also hung across the inside of the doors to help exclude the draughts, but, although they were closed as soon as possible, the cold night air had already been admitted.

On the ground the postman would recover the bags from the wayside net and lower away the net frame to its out of use position. The standards would be turned away from the track and locked out of use by padlock and chain. He was provided with a ground hut, in which a warning bell was housed, or in some cases a telephone. A store of pouches for future exchanges was also kept there. From the relative safety of this hut, the postman was able to watch the exchange. If a pouch was not received when expected or if it appeared that one was not successfully snatched by the train, a check was to be made along the line for 400 yards either side of the apparatus. In general it was the rule that the same number of bags should be exchanged at the apparatus point on every occasion. If this was not done the TPO staff were to make it known to the ground staff by a note included in the first of the bags, which incidentally were numbered with chalk on the exterior, often along with the point of destination. If a pouch broke open during the exchange, a search had to be made for any loose correspondence when the line was safe, and if necessary the local platelayers could be called out. On one occasion even divers were called to recover a pouch from the bottom of a canal!

The pouches were made of thick leather, consisting of a main body with four flaps designed to fold round the mail bags. The contents of a bag were carefully packed into a special mail bag, type 8B, which was an exchange bag made of thicker material than usual and with a black line around it acting as a load line. In the 1890s various TPOs had a number of bags allocated to them which were so marked. One or more bags could be packed into a pouch with the two side flaps being pulled round and secured by straps. The top and bottom flaps would then be pulled over and secured by the suspension strap. The pouches themselves in general weighed 20 lbs when made up. They had to be no more than ten inches thick and weigh no more than 60 lbs when despatched from the train while those collected from the ground had a maximum limit of only 50 lbs. All the straps had to be tied so that they held the contents from moving during the exchange but were not so tight as to damage them. It was possible to bundle empty pouches and the straps together and exchange these where a working imbalance occurred.

The exchange of mails at speed called for considerable care and alertness combined with valuable experience. The knowledge of the exact position of the train in the darkness was essential, especially in bad weather. As the point to point timings of the trains decreased so did the need for exchanges until the night of 4th October 1971 when the last exchange took place at Penrith. (It was not only pouches that came out from the coach on that occasion!) Increased use of road transport, mechanised sorting and the impracticability of using the apparatus with the faster train speeds resulted in the end of this fascinating aspect of railway operation.

In 1972 the Post Office offered preservation societies the chance to purchase some of the redundant equipment. This was taken up by the Great Western Society who in 1973 erected wayside apparatus at Didcot together with a ground hut recovered from Leighton Buzzard later that year. During 1979 restoration of the TPO van No. 814 allowed a reintroduction of exchanges to take place on 11th August 1979 and before the public on 29th September at the then only working apparatus point in the country.

A made up pouch ready for dispatch. *Author's collection*

The 'down' Bristol-Penzance TPO approaching the lineside apparatus at Totnes on 15th December 1911. *British Railways*

With the restoration of apparatus working following the Second World War the re-sited apparatus point at Swindon receives a slow speed test. *Post Office*

American and Canadian mails coming ashore from a tender directly into one of the 70 ft stowage vans, No. 874, at Plymouth Millbay in March 1937.
British Transport Docks Board, Millbay

CHAPTER THREE

OCEAN MAILS

THE Ocean Mails probably owes much of its fame to the epic run by the *City of Truro* on 9th May 1904. This popular title, emblazoned on some of the parcels and stowage vans, is misleading in connection with the TPOs as services for the arriving and departing liners not only included Plymouth, but, for a short period from 1909-14, Fishguard and Avonmouth, neither of which developed long term liner traffic of any significance. The TPO was actually named the 'Plymouth and Bristol TPO (Foreign Mails)' and dated from the end of the 1860s.

In 1867 the Post Office had taken over control of overseas mail contracts from the Admiralty and by 1869 transferred the sorting of mails from the West Indies, previously carried out on the packet boats, to a TPO to run between Plymouth and Bristol. A handstamp thought to have been first used on the mails from the Mediterranean packet *China* appeared as early as 1859, but this was more likely to have been used on the packet or tender than on a train.

The railway had been used for taking the West Indian mails from Falmouth to London on 21st June 1842 when the mails were to be taken from Falmouth, via Taunton, to connect with the 'Special Day Mail' from Bristol. If there was no train available at Taunton to connect with the mail then a locomotive and coach were to be hired to take the mails forward. However, this does not seem to have been a regular event!

Initially both the South Devon Railway Company and the GWR were asked to provide sorting arrangements in a carriage set aside for the West Indian mails. The service commenced on 26th August 1869 although the first handstamp recorded was used on 11th September 1874. The service seems to have worked under a number of different titles depending upon the origin or destination of the mails such as 'Special Cape & West Indian Mails' or the 'Special American Mails'. Sorting on the train ceased in the mid 1920s, but the carriage of mails from Plymouth to Paddington continued until the last train in 1963. The title of 'Special' here refers to the train as a special having no timetabled schedule. It was run as required on the arrival of the liners at Plymouth.

The eventual development of Plymouth Millbay Docks was wholly directed towards the rapid transfer of passengers and mails between the liners anchored in Plymouth Sound and the London trains.

An early link between the Great Western and Millbay was the arrival of the *Sirius* on the 21st July 1838 returning on her second voyage from New York. It was hired by the 'Liverpool Party' of the GWR to race against Brunel's *Great Western* (hired by the 'Bristol Party') in

An 'up' Ocean Mails Special with mails and passengers passes West Drayton hauled by 4–6–0 No. 2907 *Lady Disdain*.
L & GRP, courtesy David & Charles

The Great Western Railway docks and dry dock, Millbay. This view of the docks was taken after the Second World War when the liner tenders returned to the port. *Sir Richard Grenville* and *Sir John Hawkins* are berthed alongside the Princess Royal pier and Brunel's pontoon while *Sir Walter Raleigh* is alongside the Millbay pier. All tenders have new mooring lines as does the pontoon! Hardly any passenger coaches are visible and wagon loads of imported timber from two ships have been spread around the quays. The exit via North Road is past the goods shed where a loco is shunting. During the war the GWR lost more coaches in Millbay due to bombing than anywhere else. *British Transport Docks Board, Millbay*

The newly installed electric conveyor undergoing trials with a stowage van on 12th March 1937.
British Transport Docks Board, Millbay

an attempt to discredit him and so regain control of the GWR.

The original docks were commenced in 1840 by a local man, Thomas Gill, with the erection of a pier. This was soon expanded in 1846 when the Plymouth Great Western Dock Company was formed. Although this had nothing to do with the GWR at the time as the Railway Companies were by law only to engage in railway business and none other, the dock company had appointed I. K. Brunel as their engineer in planning and expanding the docks. Thomas Gill had backed Brunel's Atmospheric Railway but when it failed he went bankrupt and had to leave the dock management. Despite the support of some £50,000 from the South Devon Railway (whose original headquarters were at Millbay), the Bristol & Exeter Railway and the GWR, the dock company suffered continuing financial troubles. By 1857 the inner floating dock and a 367 ft dry dock had been completed, to a width of 80 ft, to accommodate paddle steamers but considerable havoc was wrought to the inner dock gates during a storm in October that year, causing more expenditure. The deficit continued to mount until the GWR absorbed the South Devon Railway and the dock company in 1878 after which matters began to improve.

The development of Millbay docks was restricted by the lack of deep water berths. This led to the eventual decline of traffic which passed instead to Southampton. The docks could only accept boats of 21 ft draught which meant that all liners had to be met by tenders on anchoring in the Sound.

Plymouth had long been an emigration port but liner passenger traffic began in the 1850s when Millbay station opened and the Cape Mail Union Line commenced operation. On 15th September 1857 the 530 ton steamer *Dane* took passengers and mail for Cape Town. On her return to Plymouth on 6th January 1858, 10,687 letters and 3,761 newspapers were landed, and two years later, on another call, she brought 200 sacks of mail. From around this period the quantity of mails steadily increased with the Post Office taking over control of the steam mail contracts in 1867. In January 1882 P & O vessels began calling at Plymouth.

Previously passenger trains had been platformed at Millbay station and passengers were left to walk or take a cab to or from the quay, but from January 1882 they were brought by train right down to the quay opposite the customs house. Initially passengers were charged 6d each for landing but this was soon abolished and instead the liner operators were charged for the use of the tenders. Joint steamer and railway tickets could be purchased at a cheaper rate, the first class Plymouth-Paddington fare costing 30/- while the third class was 15/-.

The development of the docks continued with the extension of one of the piers in 1890 using a pontoon originally employed in the construction of the Saltash Bridge. Later in 1902 as the traffic increased, Trinity Pier was also extended and in 1903 the American Line's boats began calling, requiring two tenders for each ship, one for passengers and one for mail. Following the 1923 Grouping when the GWR absorbed the South Wales Docks, it formed the largest dock undertaking in the world.

Christmas had always brought record amounts of mail and trans-ocean mail is no exception. Christmas week in 1912 brought a record of 9,026 bags of mail landed from the following:

A large quantity of Special American Mails comes ashore from the tender of *Sir John Hawkins* at Millbay.
British Transport Docks Board, Millbay

Ship	*Line*	*Bags*
Nieuw Amsterdam	Holland America	3,436
Kaiserin Augusta Victoria	Hamburg America	1,454
Kronprinzessin Cecilia	Norddentscher Lloyd	155
Oceanic	White Star Line	548
President Grant	Holland America	21
St. Paul	America Line	3,412

Previous record years had been 1910 with 7,458 bags, and 1911 with 8,260 bags of mail landed.

The year 1913 was to see even more mail pass through, with 26,000,000 letters being handled, made up of arrivals of 2,300 bags from India and Australia and 6,300 bags from America and Canada, mostly aboard the *Mauretania.*

On 20th December 1913 the *New York* (America Line) dropped anchor in the Sound at 3.30 p.m. with 4,654 bags of mail. Three of the tenders were used, two for mail and one for passengers, the mails being transferred to a ten coach Ocean Mails special which departed at 5.30 p.m. It was divided at Bristol for London and elsewhere in the country. Earlier in the day the White Star liner *Olympic* had arrived with 2,070 bags of mail which had also required the running of a special Ocean Mails train to London. Passengers aboard the *Olympic* included the American General H. D. Hamilton, who had crossed the Atlantic for his health and was to return the following day aboard the *Carmania.*

It was the *Olympic* which had the dubious honour of being the first liner which the tenders could not serve within the breakwater due to the rough seas on her arrival on 11th February 1914. The tender *Sir Walter Raleigh* had attempted to disembark the first and second class passengers with no success, while the *Sir Richard Grenville* had made two attempts to offload the heavy baggage, which was eventually completed. The *Sir Francis Drake* was to have handled the mails with the *Smeaton* taking off the silver coin traffic, all of which instead had to travel on to Le Havre, the next port of call, as the liner departed at 6.30 a.m. without waiting for calmer waters.

Plymouth Sound has often seen a large number of liners. On 14th October 1914, for instance, 32 liners were at anchor and on other occasions five liners arrived from New York. They were the *Paris*, the *Olympic,* the *Rotterdam,* the *Columbus* and the *President Harding*, all of which had sailed on the same day.

The importance of the traffic to the GWR is indicated by their building special coaches for the service.

A pool of coaches was kept at Old Oak Common for the exclusive use of the Ocean Mails. The 1895 roster shows four

Mails and passengers' luggage being offloaded from one of the tenders onto hand trolleys and wagons of the 2 ft 6 ins narrow gauge which ran round the quay. Mails were passed directly to the waiting coaches, but passengers' luggage was first scrutinized in the customs hall behind the photographer. *British Transport Docks Board, Millbay*

All the tenders had large open decks for handling mail, passengers' luggage being carried on the aft deck if there was room. The electrically operated conveyor installed in March 1937 required the modification of the forward deck rails of the tenders to accept it. The tenders berthed closer to the main quay so that bags could be transferred to the waiting vans. A loco would move to line up a door with the conveyor end throughout the operation. The record quantity, 3,476 bags of mail weighing 52 tons, was passed in 2½ hours from tender to train including checking and sorting the bags. Outgoing mails were also handled in the same manner, being despatched to the departing liner at the last possible minute. Here a 'Castle' class 4–6–0 waits at the head of the stowage vans while a large shipment of mails from *Sir Walter Raleigh* is loaded onto the train. When loading was completed the vans were pulled forward to join the rest of the train which is in the platform road to the left.

British Railways

40 ft PBVs numbered 862-865 running with a letter sorting carriage. By 1903 Nos. 862 and 863 were rostered, possibly with additional PBVs, and by 1915 six vans were employed, two letter sorting carriages, No. 837 of 1904 and No. 836, with four stowage vans Nos. 821–4. No. 837 was the famous slip coach which, paired with No. 863, was usually slipped at Bedminster with the mails for Bristol and the north. In latter years the mails were carried in standard PBVs allocated to the service rather than special vans or postal vehicles as no sorting was carried out on the trains. With the development of the corridor train, sets were formed for the major services including the ocean liner traffic. The Super Saloons were built with this traffic in mind. A large number of special stowage and luggage vans were built to deal with the mails from Plymouth and other ports. The competition with the L & SW Railway and the effort to reach London first was another indication of the importance of this profitable traffic. The most famous incident concerning the Ocean Mails from Plymouth was without doubt the record run of the *City of Truro*. The GWR had agreed with the LSWR to split the traffic between them, the GWR to handle the mails while the LSWR handled the passengers. What was to develop from this agreement was to eclipse the races to the north completely in engineering skills but was to be brought to a complete stop one dark night at Salisbury in disaster.

The rivalry between the two companies started in the early months of 1904. The GWR's fast running on this service was not unusual as with the arrival of the Hamburg-American Line's ship on 20th December 1895 when Paddington was reached in 4 hours 27 minutes. There are mentions of earlier high speed runs by broad gauge locomotives with very light loads. One of these trains was involved in the Norton Fitzwarren accident on 11th November 1890. Perhaps the start of these 1904 races was the arrival of the America Line's *St. Louis* in the early hours of 9th April. She anchored in the Sound, so beginning the race by both companies to have the mails and the passengers in London as soon as possible and before the other company. The GWR with the mails arrived in Paddington nineteen minutes before the LSWR passengers reached Waterloo. On 23rd April the LSWR won the laurels when they were first home, despite a compulsory stop at the GWR's station at Exeter St. David's.

The *City of Truro's* famous run was not a spontaneous event, but the result of careful preparation by a very publicity conscious company. These attempts, which were not a test of locomotive power, were aimed at taking the mails from the great liners to London by the quickest service over the fastest railway route. It appears these attempts had been in progress for some months and the run of 9th May 1904 was to be among the last. The run on 7th May had not provided the expected results even though special preparations had been made.

The North German Lloyd Company's liner *S.S. Kronprinz Wilhelm* had departed from New York at 3.00 pm on 3rd May, arriving in Plymouth Sound at 8.00 am on the 9th, a crossing of 5 days 21 hours 58 minutes. A number of passengers disembarked, some of whom were to travel by the second special from Plymouth at 9.49 am, arriving in Paddington at 2.12 pm (4 hrs. 24 mins.). The liner departed upon the rest of her voyage for Cherbourg and Bremen.

Meanwhile an exceptionally heavy shipment of between 1085 and 1300 bags of mail from New Zealand and Australia (via San Francisco) and America had been transferred aboard the new tender, *The Cheshire*, which was in use for the first time. It left for the Trinity Pier of the Great Western Docks at 8.30 am, the mail bags on board being separated for their various destinations. One source states that there were 998 bags for forwarding, mainly to London, those for South Wales, the Midlands and the north being placed in the last vehicle of the train.

The generally held concept that the train was carrying a quantity of gold bullion or specie seems unlikely as there are no records of any such shipment being made to the Bank of England or other major bullion house.

Although it has been generally believed that the train's formation was of five 70

On completion of her maiden trans-Atlantic voyage, the United States Line's *Washington* calls at Plymouth Sound to transfer mails to the GWR tender *Sir Walter Raleigh* in May 1933. Both *Washington* and her sister ship *Manhattan* were the fastest pair of true cabin class ships on the crossing carrying 580 cabin, 400 tourist and 150 third class passengers in accommodation of a very high standard. They were also the first pair of Atlantic ships to be built in America since *St. Louis* in 1895. In 1940, while off the English coast, she was ordered to stop by a German U-boat which intended to torpedo her. However, her Captain said he was an American ship and told the U-boat to go away, which it did! After the war she spent a few years on the Atlantic crossing, but was withdrawn in 1951. Following many years of inactivity she was scrapped in 1964.
British Transport Docks Board, Millbay

ft stowage vans including the famous slip coach, this may not be correct, as according to the Lot Book it appears the stowage vans of diagrams M9 and M10 were not completed until some months after the event in September 1904, slip coach No. 837 of M8 diagram making its first run on 26th January 1905. There is also no agreement between the various reports as to the train's formation, except to say that it would seem that clerestory sorting carriages could have been in use. A further source gives two mail vans and three passenger brake vans as being used. According to the roster book, Nos. 862 and 863 were allocated to the service and it is also recorded that for the Bristol to Paddington section the load was double the normal two coaches, as one of the mail coaches, the last vehicle in the formation, was detached at Bristol when the unscheduled locomotive change was made.

To deviate slightly here, further evidence of the preparations comes to light over this point. Special efforts were made to keep the line clear ahead of the special and in case of casual disarrangement of the locomotive, spare engines were kept in readiness at no fewer than five stations, Newton Abbot, Exeter, Taunton, Bristol and Swindon. The planned detachment of the last sorting coach at Bristol was also used to change the *City of Truro* which had used more coal than had been expected.

Along the route a number of people were noticed watching the train's progress and at Paddington the mails were extracted from the train amidst a crowd of onlookers and transferred to St. Martins-Le-Grand in Post Office vans.

From these reports it would seem this was certainly not a spontaneous event but, as previously mentioned, a planned attempt built up over a period of time with preparations being made in every section from Permanent Way to the Locomotive Department.

The actual train formation may never be established, but it seems likely that the coaches rostered to the service, Nos. 862 and 863, were present along with three 40 ft Dean brake vans or two 40 ft Dean brakes and one Diagram K17 van, possibly No. 1128. This type of formation would have allowed for a mail van to be detached and forwarded to Bristol while still allowing another with sorters aboard to proceed to London. Accommodation would then have been available for Mr. Rous-Martin plus any other GWR staff travelling with the train and not on the footplate.

Mr. O. S. Nock in his *60 Years of Express Running* and his *Speed Records of British Railways* gives a full and well documented account of the locomotive workings. Apart from the 102.3 mph record descent of Wellington Bank, another record was established on the second part of the journey, that of 71.3 mph for the start to stop speed record for the British Isles, which was only beaten by the Great Western's 'Cheltenham Flyer' in 1929. Another feat worthy of note was the average 57.6 mph between Totnes and Newton Abbot (a little risky?). The full story may never be known but it is certainly a fine publicity achievement as even today it is remembered and reflected upon.

The fierce competition between the rival companies ended in tragedy on the morning of 1st July 1906, the day the GWR opened the Castle Cary route to west. At 1.57 a.m. a regular Stonehouse Pool to Waterloo express conveying passengers from the America Line's *New York* was derailed at over 70 mph, killing 24 of its 43 passengers. The train of five 8-wheeled vehicles hauled by 'L12' class 4–4–0 No. 421, running under clear signals, left the rails at the eastern end of Salisbury station, on a 30 mph restricted left hand curve, hitting the rear end of a five van milk train. Three first class coaches of the passenger train and the five milk vans of the milk train were destroyed, killing the driver and fireman of the express, the guard of the milk train and the fireman of a light engine standing at the platform, whose driver was badly scalded. Ironically the express loco escaped with such minor damage that it ran back to Nine Elms on its own wheels!

So ended the race and eventually in May 1910 the LSWR entered into a pooling agreement with the GWR for operating the trains for both mails and passengers.

The fast running of the Ocean Mails continued on the GWR and when in 1924 the *Mauretania* broke her own Blue Riband Atlantic record from New York to Plymouth in 4 days 21 hours 57 minutes, the GWR were keen to complete the journey in style, arriving at Paddington in 3 hours 57 minutes behind No. 4078 *Pembroke Castle.* (Cunard were not impressed with the LSWR's running from Southampton to Waterloo during this period). The fastest run on the GWR was 3 hours 37 minutes with a five coach train of 171 tons hauled by No. 5069 *Isambard Kingdom Brunel.*

Despite the interruption of the First World War, passengers and mail had continued to increase. 1930 saw a record 789 liners calling at Plymouth landing 307,912 bags of mail, and in 1931 the Ocean or Super Saloon coaches were introduced on the GWR boat trains. The first pair, Nos. 9111 and 9112, were used for a party of guests of the French Line travelling from Le Havre to London on the occasion of the maiden voyage of the *Colombie.*

Between 29th May and 31st December 1930 the GWR had experimented with Pullman coaches from Plymouth but were dissatisfied with them and built their own superior stock. The Pullmans were subsequently withdrawn from the GWR and transferred to the Southern Railway's Southampton-Waterloo ocean liner service.

By 1938, with the threat of the Second World War looming, travel was declining, although passenger landings remained above 30,000 a year. Following the war, a general decline in seaborne traffic began, even though 437,000 bags of mail were still landed in 1949. In 1947 mail contracts ceased to be given to the steamer companies as air traffic became faster and better managed. The number of liners and the amount of mail declined until the last year of operations, 1962, when 82 liners called but only 6,425 passengers were landed at Plymouth.

FISHGUARD

Attempts were made to develop Fishguard and Avonmouth as liner terminals, both without success. The GWR wanted to develop the short sea route to Ireland, so breaking the LNWR's monopoly of the Irish traffic. This was coupled with a desire to capture the liner traffic from Liverpool and establish a gateway to Europe. A whole hillside had to be blasted away to provide a site for the station, power station and to provide material for the breakwater. A further site was also required for the hotel above the station. An estimated 2,000,000 tons of solid rock was displaced and in one single blast some 113,000 tons were dislodged with great blocks of 5,000 tons broken out from the cliff.

The first services to Ireland commenced in April 1908, soon after which the first liners started to call at Fishguard as the mails could be in London up to 24 hours earlier than by the older route via Liver-

The S.S. *Mauretania* off Fishguard on 30th August 1909 with the tender *Smeaton* alongside receiving mails while passengers for Liverpool watch from the boat deck. *Great Western Society collection*

S.S. *Mauretania* off Fishguard after arrival with two tenders waiting for her to anchor and settle. A large number of people gathered on the hill above the harbour where they had a panoramic view of the day's special events. The rock blasted away from the hill for the station site, together with material from a local quarry, was used to form the breakwater.

Great Western Society collection

More and more mail from the *Mauretania* being loaded onto *Smeaton* while *Sir Francis Drake* comes alongside astern to collect the passengers.
Great Western Society collection

pool. The White Star liners already called at Holyhead so to better this the Cunard began calling at Fishguard.

The GWR pulled out all the stops for this traffic which commenced on 30th August 1909. At 1.15 pm the Cunard liner *Mauretania* arrived off Fishguard and anchored to transfer mail and passengers to the waiting tenders, having sailed from New York on the 25th. On arrival the liner was met by three tenders, the *Smeaton* for the 800 bags of mail, the *Sir Francis Drake* for the passengers and the *Great Western* for passengers' luggage, all of which had been detached from the fleet at Plymouth specially for this traffic. For the passengers' onward journey to London, the GWR provided three special trains with special coach destination boards proclaiming 'Cunard Ocean Express, Fishguard–London'. A number of Dover destination boards had also been prepared but only a small number of passengers wished to travel through to the continent so other arrangements were made. No ordinary trains were run from the station and the general public were excluded except by special permit. The first departure was a special Ocean Mails which left from the Ocean Quay extension

At least three photographers were present to record this first call of the Cunard liner to Fishguard. The GWR had made special efforts to attract traffic to the port and away from Holyhead. With all the passengers and mails aboard, the tenders leave the liner, which was heaving anchor for the final leg to Liverpool. *Great Western Society collection*

Having returned to the protection of the massive breakwater, *Sir Frances Drake* has berthed at the quayside ahead of another GWR vessel. The disembarking passengers are making their way straight into the station and the awaiting train. How customs procedures have changed!

Great Western Society collection

station which lay half a mile beyond the main station. The train consisted of three vans as far as Cardiff and thence two to Paddington, hauled by No. 4023 *King George* which had taken over at Cardiff from No. 3381 *Maine.* The commercial department of the GWR had arranged massive publicity covering the arrival of the liner and the running of the trains, each passenger receiving an attractively bound guide to the route. People travelled from miles around Fishguard to see both the *Mauretania* and the special trains, crowds assembling at many stations and level crossings along the route. One newspaper reported that Paddington was besieged by 'railwayists'!

The timings of this special were as follows:

Cunard Special No. 1

Liner dropped anchor		1.15 p.m.
Ocean Quay station	dept.	2.08 p.m.
Fishguard Harbour station		2.12 p.m.
Cardiff	arr.	4.19 p.m.
Loco changed to 4–6–0 No. 4023 *King George*. 1 van detached.		
	dept.	4.22 p.m.
Paddington	arr.	6.40 p.m.

The following year, after another record-breaking voyage to New York and back, the *Mauretania* arrived off Fishguard on 22nd December 1910 with 3,177 bags of mail and 598 passengers wishing to travel onward by rail. The GWR ran five specials, the first of which, chartered by the *Daily Mail*, departed at 11.30 pm, and arrived in Paddington 271 minutes later (4 hours 31 minutes) achieving an average speed of 57.8 mph. The other four all departed between 11.48 and 1.15 am, the first bound for Dover and the continent via Reading while the remainder went to Paddington.

The mails having been offloaded from *Smeaton* were loaded aboard the Cunard Special No. 1 at the Ocean station at Fishguard where 'Atbara' class 4–4–0 No. 3381 *Maine* stands ready with its three coach special for Paddington. *Great Western Society collection*

Having offloaded mails at the Ocean Quay, *Smeaton* with Post Office and company staff returns to the Harbour Quay. The Ocean Quay berth and station can be seen behind the tender. A number of coal barges can also be seen in the harbour. *Great Western Society collection*

No. 837 (Diagram M8), the 70 ft slip stowage van, and No. 863 (Diagram L10), a Foreign Mails van, being slipped at Bedminster, Bristol, at 69 mph on an 'up' Ocean Mails Special in 1905.
British Railways

An unidentified 'Star' class 4–6–0 on a Fishguard to Paddington mail train. This may have been a Cunard Special. *British Railways*

Traffic from Fishguard continued to increase with Cunard calling six to eight times a month. Each call required the running of three or four trains, including a mail special but after the First World War Cunard and White Star line moved their services from Liverpool to Southampton. Fishguard consequently fell into a slump from which it has slowly recovered in recent years with the expansion of trade with Ireland. The problems at Fishguard centred round the lack of deep water berths and, as at Plymouth, the need to transfer mails and passengers by tender. The GWR had obtained powers to overcome this but the First World War stopped the work being put into practice and the Atlantic dream faded with the expansion of Southampton and Le Havre.

AVONMOUTH

Attempts at Avonmouth centred mostly on the West Indian traffic as the port was chosen as the UK terminal for the Imperial Direct West Indian Mail service with fortnightly sailings from Avonmouth to Kingston, Jamaica. New dock facilities did encourage trade but none of the great trans-Atlantic liners came near the Bristol Channel let alone Avonmouth. The liners engaged were mostly fruit boats with only 100 or so passengers. Special trains for the passengers and occasionally the mails could be ordered by the shipping lines in advance if required. The last special was run on 26th August 1964 for the sailing of the *Camito* to Trinidad, the coaches being attached to the Paddington-Bristol Express and worked forward specially.

A full house for the arrival of the second new *Sir John Hawkins* alongside the Millbay Pier in 1929. Her port of registration was soon to be changed from London to Plymouth. *Sir Richard Grenville* is alongside the Princess Royal Pier, while *Sir Walter Raleigh* and *Sir Francis Drake* are on the far side of the pontoon.

The rolling stock in the station roads included an Ocean Mails full brake, some 70 ft stock and the royal clerestory roofed 1897 composite No. 7413 (Lot 831). The last mentioned was a regular visitor to Millbay. *British Transport Docks Board, Millbay*

A 'Castle' class 4–6–0 passing Pyle Hill sidings, Bristol, on arrival with the 12.10 p.m. from Penzance c.1936. This train ran to Newport and on to the north conveying the Cardiff-Crewe TPO which arrived at Crewe at 11.22 p.m. The first coach, an L22 diagram Sorting Van, forms the Plymouth to Bristol TPO working. The remainder of the train comprises an assortment of Great Western and other companies' vehicles with clerestories, toplights and vans. *G. H. Soole, courtesy of the National Railway Museum, York*

CHAPTER FOUR

COACH ALLOCATIONS, TRAIN FORMATIONS & TIMINGS

COACHES were allocated to various services in set formations running to the times required by the Post Office. The following tables give a broad insight into the methods employed by the GWR in the working arrangements relating to its coaches, an aspect which has changed radically in the past 20 years with coaching stock covering a far higher mileage and greater economic utilization. In fact the working of coaching stock was far more complex than any loco diagram.

Most of the TPO coaches were built with a particular service in mind and spent the majority of their lives upon these services. Three coaches were allocated to each working to provide two in traffic and a third as spare to stand in for traffic failures or cover vehicles away for works attention. The spare was kept at a depot local to the service and in most cases rotated with the service stock. When problems arose, it was sometimes possible to find an out of course vehicle from another service, but this often led to a shortage of sorting space or apparatus. The best example of this occurred on the reintroduction of the TPOs following the Second World War in 1945 where stock was initially rostered because of its operating condition rather than its suitability to the service.

The formation of the trains was far more the concern of the GWR than the Post Office except in the operation of the Great Western TPO which was and still is a 'Special' TPO. The other TPO services run by the GWR for the Post Office were marshalled initially for the Post Office and then for the railway company's convenience in logical order. Under the agreement with the Post Office, TPO coaches were placed at the head of a train and, by virtue of their side corridor connections, apart from the rest of the train. Other coaches in the train would be entirely at the operating requirements of the GWR although not always to the needs of the passengers. Unlike the working of normal passenger coaches, the working of a TPO vehicle was relatively straightforward, the coach working back on the next return service to the start point or out of use with a service train where the TPO service was one way only. The complexity of passenger coach rostering is illustrated by a set of four coaches which worked 12 services over a 6 day period before returning to its start point.

The example is taken from the Summer workings of 1903 and, although a little extreme, highlights the detailed planning involved.

4.20 p.m. Basingstoke to Birmingham
(Van 3rd, Compo, Compo, Van 3rd)

Day 1
4.20 p.m. Basingstoke – Birmingham
8.25 p.m. Birmingham – Wolverhampton

Day 2
1.45 p.m. Wolverhampton – Birmingham
3.00 p.m. Birmingham – Leamington

Day 3
10.15 a.m. Leamington – Oxford
12.35 a.m. Oxford – Didcot
1.15 p.m. Didcot – Cheltenham

Day 4
6.45 a.m. Cheltenham – Cardiff
7.30 a.m. Cardiff – Carmarthen

Day 5
7.15 a.m. Carmarthen – Swansea
9.50 a.m. Swansea – Swindon

Day 6
6.05 p.m. Swindon – Reading

Day 7
3.18 p.m. Reading – Basingstoke
coupled to
3.18 p.m. Reading – Basingstoke*
(similar formation but 6-wheeled stock)

*This set originally formed part of the train from Basingstoke and was detached at Reading West, forwarded to Reading General at 4.59 p.m.

The amount of running in passenger service was comparatively little as the coaches spent the majority of their time standing in the carriage sidings. To work this non frontline service, the GWR had tied up 7 sets, a total of 28 coaches, hence the vast numbers of vehicles needed to run all the services. In today's operations some HST sets complete three return Paddington – Swansea trips a day. The train given above had an interesting history as in the 1905 roster it formed the Weymouth to Birmingham train with coaches from Bournemouth to Birkenhead, Bradford* and Newcastle*. (*Great Central stock). By 1929 the service had been reduced to Portsmouth Harbour to Birmingham only, and even today a similar train can be found in the timetable.

As already established, the running of the TPO trains was to the requirements of the Post Office who laid down the train times under the various schedules. The TPOs were run as part of a wider network of services, interconnecting in an effort to secure the earliest deliveries. The GW TPO still carries mails for forward transmission to the Midlands and the north (Liverpool, Manchester and York).

Since the timetable was first cast there has been little alteration in its basic framework. Increasing speeds have given rise to faster point to point timings such that the down GW TPO now leaves later from Paddington than it did one hundred years ago, so allowing later collections of mail to be forwarded to the west, although the connection time at Bristol has remained virtually the same.

Certainly the timings of the TPOs have little relevance to the requirements of the passengers that may use the services of the passenger section of the train or to normal railway operations. The running of a TPO did not call for spectacular loco work but for a steady and regular service. The knock-on effect of a late TPO would mean late mail deliveries to many parts of the country. Early running could seriously affect the apparatus working with postmen failing to meet the TPO at wayside locations. It was therefore vital that the TPO kept to the times laid out in the working arrangements regardless of any permanent way restrictions or late running of previous trains; even weather should not affect the service. Timing was also important for the postman at the lineside apparatus. He had to be ready some 15 minutes beforehand, but if an ordinary passenger or goods train were to pass while a bag was swung out ready for the 'Mail' it could have serious consequences.

For those on the train the precise time was not of such great importance for operating the apparatus as a good deal of this work was carried out with years of experience and knowledge of apparatus locations. The GWR issued special instructions for each location as given in Appendix 3, but to quote an example from the 1907 up service, the apparatus at Grampound Road was some 300 yards east of the station: 'After leaving Truro pass through two tunnels, over two viaducts, by two platelayers huts, observe signal; fix on in a cutting; pass through the station and by signal post lower the net and extend the arms.' Even at night the train's passage through the two tunnels and across the two viaducts would be clearly heard and the cutting known. The station lights would have been seen and the coach's exterior lights would have picked out the signal post as it flashed past. To miss or have the wrong location would have led to considerable damage. Apparatus has been stripped off a number of coaches by a signal post at a different location, so the ability of the loco crew to keep the TPO to its correct time path was of the utmost importance.

The Post Office did have agreements to cover the late running of TPOs either by holding for a period other trains or where required by running additional trains.

A vast selection of information came to hand during the research for this chapter and a separate volume could be written on the variations alone. However, times and rosterings for particular years have been quoted from various working books in an attempt to give a broad outline of the overall operation. To specify an individual coach running at a particular time working various apparatus points would be difficult unless an observer had recorded the whole scene. As far as is known, the dates and figures quoted are correct but variations did occur. The use of information from the early 1900s is intended to give a view of the services at a period when they were most active and most interesting.

Coach allocations have come from various roster books with some notes from the 'Working of Coaches' books used by the GWR. These have yielded the train formations and the return workings of the coaches. The times of the services have come from timetables issued by the GWR and from various working and duty books as did the apparatus workings. In many cases these did not agree with each other for the same dates!

On 21st July 1956 the 'up' Plymouth-Bristol TPO hauled by No. 6962 *Soughton Hall* nears the end of the long climb to Whiteball Tunnel on the Somerset-Devon border. The first coach is TPO van No. W799W followed by the usual LMS coach. *R. C. Riley*

TABLE INDEX

EXPLANATION OF GENERAL NOTES and INSTRUCTIONS

A	Brake end trailing.
B	Brake end leading.
M	Monday.
T	Tuesday.
W	Wednesday.
Th	Thursday.
F	Friday.
S	Saturday.
SS	Sunday.
O	Only.
X	Excepted.
MO	Monday only.
MTO	Mondays & Tuesdays only.
MWO	Mondays & Wednesdays only.
MTHO	Mondays & Thursdays only.
MFO	Mondays & Fridays only.
MSO	Mondays & Saturdays only.
MTTHSO	Mondays, Tuesdays, Thursdays and Saturdays only.
MWSO	Mondays, Wednesdays & Saturdays only.
MTHO	Mondays, Thursdays and Saturdays only.
FO	Fridays only.
FX	Fridays excepted.
SO	Saturdays only.
SX	Saturdays excepted.
SSO	Sundays only.
SSX	Sundays excepted.
TO	Tuesdays only.
THO	Thursdays only.
TTHSO	Tuesdays, Thursdays & Saturdays only.
WO	Wednesdays only.
WFO	Wednesdays & Fridays only.
WSO	Wednesdays & Saturdays only.
RR	Runs as required.
57	57′ coach.
60	60′ coach.
70	70′ coach.
+	Non gangwayed coach.
*	Empty stock not to be attached to these trains.

APPARATUS WORKING

D = Despatch
R = Receive

and quoted as bags despatched/received in all instances.

TABLE 'A' MAIL TRAINS January 1858

PADDINGTON – PLYMOUTH

	Down				Up		
	MAIL	MAIL	MAIL	MAIL	MAIL	MAIL	MAIL
Station	*a.m.*		*p.m.*	*a.m.*	*p.m.*	*p.m.*	*p.m.*
PADDINGTON	10.00		8.10		10.35		4.50
West Drayton	10.28		–		–		–
Slough	10.40		–		–		4.10
Maidenhead	10.52		8.45		–		4.00
Twyford	11.10		–		–		3.40
READING	11.25		9.15		9.33		3.25
Wallingford Rd.	11.49		–		–		2.40
DIDCOT Junc.	12.04		9.45		9.05		2.25
Faringdon Rd.	12.30		10.07		8.28		1.55
SWINDON Junc.	1.10	1.12	10.45		8.00		1.25
Chippenham	1.38	'B'	11.18		7.15		'B'
Bath	2.03		11.50		6.40		↑
BRISTOL	2.50		12.40	7.50	5.30	12.25	
Nailsea	3.05		–	8.08	5.10	–	
Yatton	3.15		–	8.18	4.55	–	
Banwell	3.22		–	8.26	–	–	
Weston-S-Mare	3.31		1.25	8.35	4.40	11.40	
Highbridge	3.47		–	8.53	4.25	–	
BRIDGWATER	4.03		1.50	9.10	4.14	11.15	
Durston	4.14		–	9.20	4.00	–	
Taunton	4.26		2.15	9.30	3.48	10.50	
Wellington	4.42		2.30	9.45	3.33	10.33	
Tiverton Junc.	5.07		2.50	10.08	3.17	10.12	
Cullompton	5.15		2.55	10.14	3.10	10.07	
Hele	5.30		–	10.25	3.00	–	
EXETER a.	5.50		3.20	10.40	d. 2.45	9.45	
d.	6.15		3.30	10.50	a. 2.30	9.35	
Starcross	6.40		3.45	11.10	2.07	9.12	
Dawlish	6.50		3.54	11.20	1.57	9.02	
Teignmouth	7.00		4.03	11.30	1.47	8.52	
Newton	7.12		4.17	11.50	1.35	8.40	
Totnes	7.50		4.40	12.15	1.06	8.10	
Brent	8.13		–	12.38	–	–	
Kingsbridge Rd.	8.20		–	12.44	12.45	7.50	
Ivybridge	8.30		5.10	12.53	12.35	7.42	
Plympton	8.48		5.27	1.08	12.15	7.22	
PLYMOUTH	9.05	↓	5.45	1.25	12.00	7.10	

NOTES appertaining to the October 1886 working timetable

9.00 p.m. Down from Paddington (BG train)

Apparatus worked at the following:
Yatton, Hutton Bridge (between Worle Junction and Uphill Junction), Wellington, Tiverton, Cullompton.
Speed to be reduced to 35 mph at the apparatus point at Tiverton Junction & Cullompton.

6.15 a.m. Down from Bristol (BG train)

Apparatus worked at the following:
Bourton, Nailsea, Huish, Wellington, Cullompton.

9.00 a.m. Down from Paddington (BG train)

As per the 9.00 p.m. train.

10.00 a.m. Up from Penzance to Paddington

Apparatus worked at the following:
Cullompton, Tiverton Junction, Wellington, Highbridge, Hutton Bridge, Yatton, Nailsea and Bourton.

5.00 p.m. from Penzance

As per the 10.00 a.m. departure but not at Nailsea and Bourton.

A Post Office Trolley will be worked over the old Weston branch line from a point near the gas works sidings to a siding at the old Weston Junction for the purposes of conveying the Weston-Super-Mare mail bags to and from the Up & Down Night Mails.

TABLE 'A' MAIL TRAINS January 1858

SWINDON – WEST WALES

		Down			Up
		MAIL	MAIL		MAIL
		a.m.	*p.m. 'B'*		*a.m. 'B'*
SWINDON Junc.			1.12		1.13
Purton			1.22		–
Minety			1.32		–
Tetbury Rd.			1.48		12.40
Stroud			2.14		12.05
GLOUCESTER	a.		2.40	d.	11.40
	d.	2.15	3.00	a.	10.47**
Grange Court		–	3.20		–
Newnham		2.38	3.30		10.20
Gatcombe		–	3.40		–
Lydney		2.56	3.53		–
Woolaston		–	4.02		10.00
Chepstow		3.12	4.20		9.45
Portskewett		–	4.32		–
Magor		–	4.43		–
Llanwern		–	4.58		–
NEWPORT		3.40	5.12		9.15
Marshfield		–	5.27		–
CARDIFF		4.04	5.50		8.48
Ely		–	5.55		–
St. Fagans		–	6.02		–
Llantrisant		4.27	6.17		8.27
Pencoed		–	6.25		–
Bridgend		4.46	6.40		8.08
Pyle		–	6.53		–
Port Talbot		5.12	7.09		7.45
Briton Ferry		–	7.19		–
Neath		5.25	7.32		7.31
Llansamlet		–	7.43		–
Landore		–	–		–
SWANSEA		5.55	7.40		7.15
Gower Rd .		–	8.19		–
Loughor		–	8.24		–
Llanelly		6.25	8.34		6.40
Pembrey		–	8.45		–
Kidwelly		6.45	8.56		6.20
Ferryside		6.58	9.08		6.05
CARMARTHEN		7.15	9.23		5.52
St. Clears		7.28	9.40		5.29
Whitland		7.40	9.55		5.17
Narberth Rd.		7.55	10.09		5.02
Clarbeston Rd.		8.15	10.29		4.47
Haverfordwest		8.30	10.44		4.32
Johnston		8.45	11.00		4.22
MILFORD HAVEN	a.	8.55	11.10	d.	4.07
		p.m.	*p.m.*		*p.m.*

** On Sundays runs to Gloucester only.

TABLE 'B' MAIL TRAINS 1898 TIMETABLE

	MAIL NO. 1						MAIL NO. 2						MAIL NO. 4			MAIL NO. 3					
	DOWN	D	R	UP	D	R	DOWN	D	R	UP	D	R	DOWN	D	R	DOWN	D	R	UP	D	R
PADDINGTON	9.00			4.05			5.30			5.55											
Southall	9.16	3	3	3.48	4	4	5.46	1	1	5.38	1	1									
West Drayton	9.20	1	1	3.43	1	1	5.50	2	2												
Slough	9.25	2	3	3.37	2	1q	5.55	6	6a												
Maidenhead	9.30	2	3b	3.26	3	2	6.00	2	1	5.20	1	2									
READING																					
Cholsey	10.12	4	4c	2.50	4	4n	6.45	1	1	4.50	1	1									
DIDCOT																					
Steventon																					
Wantage Rd.	10.32	2	2	2.27	1	1															
SWINDON																					
Wootton Bassett										3.54	1	1									
CHIPPENHAM										3.41	4	4									
Corsham										3.36	1	1				BRISTOL AND EXETER DAY MAIL					
BATH																					
BRISTOL	12.13						7.48			3.00											
	12.23												12.07			d. 6.15			a. 7.24		
Flax Bourton							SEE TABLE 2									6.29	1	0			
Nailsea																6.31	1	0			
Yatton	12.41	4	1d	12.18	1	3							12.24	1	1	6.34	3e	1	7.04	1	3
Hewish																6.38	1	1			
Weston-S-Mare	12.50	6	2	12.09	2	6							12.27	1	1	6.42	O		6.58	1	1
Highbridge														2	2	6.53	2	2	6.48	2	2
Bridgwater	1.11												12.45	1	1	7.06	2	2	6.41	1	1
TAUNTON	1.33												13.00			7.34			6.22		
	1.38												13.05			7.41			6.21		
Wellington				11.10	5	5N							13.11	1	1	7.52	1	1	6.10	1	1
Tiverton Junc.	2.05	4	1	10.55	1	3M							13.26	1	1	8.07			6.02	1	1
Cullompton	2.15	4	1	10.48	1	4							13.30	1	1	8.15	1	1	5.58	1	1
EXETER													13.49			8.32			5.40		
													RE								
Dawlish	2.50	2	0										Carriage returns empty on the 7.48 EXETER to BRISTOL. See Table 3			PASSENGER TRAIN ↓			PASSENGER TRAIN ↑		
Teignmouth																					
NEWTON ABBOT	3.15																				
	3.22																				
Totnes	3.45	5	5																		
Brent	3.45	4	4g	8.55	2	21															
Ivybridge	3.50	2	2	8.50	1	1															
Plympton	4.00	2	2h	8.32	1	1															
PLYMOUTH	4.27															10.38	1	1	4.04	2	2
	4.40																				
Saltash																					
St. German's	4.45	1	1j	7.37	1	1															
Bodmin Road																					
Lostwithiel	5.27	1	1																		
Par																					
St. Austell																					
Grampound Rd.	6.03	3	3k																		
TRURO																					

	MAIL NO. 1					
	DOWN			UP		
TRURO						
Scorrier	6.40	2	1	5.41	1	2
Redruth						
Camborne						
Gwinear Rd.						
St. Erth						
Marazion	7.18	1	1	4.55	1	1
PENZANCE						

1901 ALTERATIONS

a 2nd ground net in use
b originally D1 R2
c drop later ceased
d reduced to 3 - 1
e reduced to 4 - 1
f Transferred to Day Mail
g 5 SO
h reduced to 1 - 1
J increased to 2 - 2
k 4 - 4 SSO
l originally 1 - 1 2nd standard SSO
0 - 4 SSO later 2 - 2 / 2 - 3 SSO
M increased to 4
N later ceased
O later 3 - 7
q increased to 3 - 2

MAIL No.	SERVICE
1.	London – Penzance Night Mail
2.	London – Bristol Sorting Carriage
3.	Bristol & Exeter Day Mail
4.	Bristol – Penzance North Mail

TABLE 1
10.10 p.m. PADDINGTON – BRISTOL – PENZANCE
Great Western T.P.O.

COACH ALLOCATIONS

Year	*Coach Nos.*	*Nets* ns	*Nets* os	*Arms* ns	*Arms* os
1903	847/8/9	1		4	
	864/5	1		4	
	782/5/6				
	850-3	1		4	
1915	834/5/6			4	
	847/8/9	1		4	2
	830/1/2		1		4
	1062-5				
	782/5/6				
	1128				
	850-3	1	1	4	4
1924	1063/4				
	850/2/3	1	1	4	4
	834/5/6	1			2
	830/1/2		1		4
1926	1062-5				
	847/9/50/2/3	1	1	4	4
	834/5/6			4	
	806/7/8	1		4	2
	830/2		1		2
1925	812/3/4	1			
	793/4/5	1		4	
	834/5/6			4	
	806/7/8	1		4	
	830/1/2		1		4

ns – near side
os – off side

October 1944 Train Formation

Van	Bristol
Van	Exeter
Van	Plymouth
Siphon G	Penzance, 4.00 a.m. ex Ply. to Pen.
Bk. Van 812/3/4	Penzance
793/4/5	Penzance
81/1125/1177	Penzance
Siphon G	Plymouth
Siphon G	Exeter
Siphon G	Exeter
Van	Torrington (Up Train only)

Summer 1945

Coach letter	
A	812/3/4
B	793/4/5
C	843/4
D	845/6
E	847/835

1.10.45 to 5.6.46

Coach letter	
A	812/3/4
B	793/4/5
C	806/7/8 **
D	848/9/798
E	796/808/835
F	81/1177/1125

****Summer 1945**

If a C or E carriage were taken out of service it was to be replaced by carriage D or from the spares 806/7/8.

1.10.45

797/798/835 were to be used as spares.

1125/6/7/8/871 could also be used as F vans.

806/7/8/835 were held at Addison Road from 7.8.45 to 14.9.45.

793/4/5 11th to 14th Sept. attached to 9.15 a.m. Paddington to Bristol arr. 12.27, returning 5.30 p.m. Bristol to Paddington arr. 8.30 p.m.

812/3/4 after 23rd Sept. to be used for final apparatus trials.

1126/7/8 to be worked as additional brake vehicles during the period.

Date	*Coach letter*	*Coach Nos.*	*Nets* ns	*Nets* os	*Arms* ns	*Arms* os
26.4.47	A	812/3/4				
	B	793/4/5				
	C	843/4/5				
	D	806/7/8				
	E	846/7/835				
1951	A	812/3/4	1	1	4	
	B	793/4/5	1		4	
	C	843/4/5				
	D	806/7/8	1		4	
	E	846/7/835				
	F	81/39/1177				

ns – near side
os – off side

June 1959

Siphon G	Penzance
812/3/4	Penzance
793/4/5	Penzance
843/4/5	Penzance
806/7/8	Penzance
846/7/35	Penzance
39/81/1177	Penzance
Siphon G	Plymouth
Siphon G	Exeter
Siphon G	Exeter for Torrington
Siphon G	Bristol

GW TPO Apparatus Working 1929 – 1939

	DOWN		*UP*	
Location	*Time*	*Pouches*	*Time*	*Pouches*
SLOUGH	10.31	R = 1 Sun, 2 Mon-Fri, 1 Sat		
WEST DRAYTON			3.34	R = 1 Sun-Fri, 1* Mon-Fri 0 Sat D = 1 Sun, 2 Mon-Fri, 0 Sat
MAIDENHEAD	10.37	R = 2	3.17	R = 1 Sun-Fri, 0 Sat 2* Sun, 4* Mon-Fri D = 4 Sun, 6 Mon-Thr 8 Fri, 0 Sat
WANTAGE ROAD	11.22	R = 1 Mon-Sat, 2 Sun D = 2 Mon/Wed/Fri/Sat		
SWINDON	11.37	R = 5 Sun, 4 Mon-Sat D = 3 + 2* Sun (1* Mon-Sat)		
CHIPPENHAM	11.55	R = 6 Sun, 4 Mon-Fri, 3 Sat D = 4 Sun-Thr, 6 Fri, 3 Sat		
BRIDGWATER	01.23	R = 1 + 4* Sun-Fri D = 6 Sun, 8 Mon-Thr 10 Fri, 0 Sat		
CULLOMPTON			10.56	R = 2 Sun, 0 Mon-Sat.
TOTNES			9.51	R = 2 Mon-Sat, 0 Sun.
ST. GERMAN'S	04.14	R = 2* Sun-Fri, 0 Sat D = 2 Sun-Fri, 0 Sat		
LISKEARD	04.25	D = 5 Mon-Fri, 4 Sat 3 Sun	8.41	R = 3 Mon-Sat, 0 Sun.
LOSTWITHIEL	04.48	D = 2 Sun-Fri		
REDRUTH	05.52	D = 7 Sun-Fri R = 1 + 4* Sun-Fri, 0 Sat	7.18	R = 2 Mon-Fri, 0 Sun
CAMBORNE	05.57	R = 1 + 3* Sun-Fri		

* – Empty pouches to balance working
R – Receive pouches
D – Despatch pouches

1946 until cessation

	DOWN
MAIDENHEAD	R = 2
SWINDON	R = 5 Sun, 4 Mon-Sat D = 3, 2* Sun, 1* Mon-Sat
CHIPPENHAM	R = 6 Sun, 4 Mon-Fri, 3 Sat D = 4 Sun-Thr, 6 Fri, 3 Sat
LISKEARD	D = 1 + 2* Sun, 3 Mon-Sat
	UP
LISKEARD	R = 3 Mon-Sat

TABLE 1 — 10.00 p.m. PADDINGTON – PENZANCE
Great Western TPO

YEAR	Train	From Paddington To	VEHICLE.		WORKING. From	WORKING. To	RETURNING BY		Due at Paddington at
1903	9 5 p.m. (Mail) *	Plymouth (North Rd.) due 70′ 4.7 a.m. (*Saturdays excepted*)	Bk. Van 1063-4 or 5	XF	Padd'ton	Penzance ...	5.10 p.m.	Penzance	4. 5 a.m.
			P. O. Carr. 851-2 or 3	XF	,,	,,	,,	,,	,,
			P. O. Carr. 834-5 or 6	XF	,,	,,	,,	,,	,,
			P. O. Carr. 847-8 or 9	X	,,	Plymouth (North Rd.)	8.30 p.m.	Plymouth (North Rd.)	,,
			P. O. Carr. 830-1 or 2	X	,,	,,	,,	,,	,,
			Van Brake...		,,	,,	,,	,,	,,
			Van 876 or 7	X	,,	Exeter	10.11 p.m.	Exeter	,,

F On from Plymouth by 10.0 p.m. Paddington.

YEAR	Train.	From Paddington To	VEHICLE.		WORKING. From	WORKING. To	RETURNING BY		Due at Paddington at	
1903	10 0 p.m. *	Pen-zance due 8.5 a.m. 70′	Bk. Van 1063-4 or 5	ES X	Pl'mouth	Penzance ...	5.10 p.m.	Penzance	4. 5 a.m.	
			P.O. Carr. 851-2 or 3	ES X	,,	,,	,,	,,	,,	
			P.O. Carr. 834-5 or 6	ES X	,,	,,	,,	,,	,,	
			Van	X SO	*Padd'ton*	*Kingswear*	*8.40 p.m.*	*Taunton ...*	*2.45 a.m.‡*	
		70′	*P.O. Carr. 830-1 or 2*	SO K	,,	*Penzance ...*	*4.30 p.m.*	*Penzance ...*	*3.50 a.m.*	*Sun.*
		70′	Van	X	,,	,,	6.55 p.m.	Tavist'k Jc.	2.15 a.m.	WG
		70′	Third	X	,,	,,	9. 0 p.m.	North Rd.	3.15 a.m.	WJ
			Sleeping Car	X	,,	,,	12. 5 a.m.	Plymouth	6.45 a.m.	Q
			Compo ...	XN	,,	,,	9. 0 p.m.	North Rd.	3.15 a.m.	WJ
			Van 3rd(3c)	X D	,,	,,	,,	,,	,,	WJ
			Van Third	X	,,	Plymouth	4. 0 p.m.	Plymouth	2.45 a.m.	
			Compo	X	,,	,,	V ,,	,,	,,	
			Third	X	,,	,,	,,	,,	,,	
			Van Third	X	,,	,,	,,	,,	,,	
			Third	X RR	,,	*Bristol ...*	—	—	—	

D This must be an open Van Third, *i.e.*, without partition in Guard's portion.
E Off 9.5 p.m. Paddington.
G Off 2.0 p.m. Penzance to Tavistock Junction.
J Off 5.10 p.m. Penzance to North Road.
K Apparatus to be on platform side of train.
N Three First and four Third Class compartments.
Q Returned to Plymouth on 9.45 a.m. Penzance, Saturdays excepted, and on Saturdays on 5.10 p.m. train throughout.
V Detached North Road and thence to Plymouth at 5.0 a.m.
W These vehicles arriving at Penzance on Sunday mornings, form 11.0 a.m. Penzance Sundays.
‡ 9.45 a.m. Kingswear to Exeter, 2.25 p.m. Exeter to Taunton.

YEAR	Train	From Paddington To	Wheels	VEHICLE	WORKING From	WORKING To	RETURNING BY		Due at Paddington at
1905 and 1919	p.m. 9 5 (Mail) *	Penzance ..	8	Brake Van....	Paddington	Penzance ...	p.m. 6 0	Penzance	a.m. 3 50
			8	Parcel Post Stg. Van.	,,	,,	,,	,,	,,
			8	Mail Tender	,,	,,	,,	,,	,,
			8	Letter Car	,,	,,	,,	,,	,,
			8	Cape Mail Ch.	,,	,,	,,	,,	,,
			8	Stowing Van	,,	,,	,,	,,	,,
			8	Brake Van ...	,,	,,	,,	,,	,,
			8	P. Post Van..	,,	Exeter ...	10 40	Exeter	,,

YEAR	Train	Wheels	VEHICLE		WORKING From	WORKING To	RETURNING BY		Due at Paddington at	
1929	**10 10** p.m. (Mail) to Penzance due 6 21 a.m. (*On Saturday nights runs to Plymouth North Road only.*) *	70	Bk. Van 1063–4 or 5 ..		Paddington	Penzance ..	6.48 p.m.	Penzance ..	3.50 a.m.	B
			P.O. Carr. 850–2 or 3 ..		,,	,,	,,	,,	,,	
			P.O. Carr. 834–5 or 6 ..		,,	,,	,,	,,	,,	
			P.O. Carr. 847–8 or 9 ..		,,	,,	,,	,,	,,	
			P.O. Carr. 830–1 or 2 ..		,,	,,	,,	,,	,,	
			Brake Van ...	+	,,	,,	,,	,,	,,	
			Siphon G	A	,,	Exeter	10.45 p.m.	Exeter	,,	
			Siphon G		,,	Bristol	11.12 a.m.	Bristol	2.55 p.m.	

A MO Siphon G not included
B Arrives Paddington 3.45 a.m.

TABLE 1 — Return Workings

YEAR	Train.	To Paddington from	Due at Paddn. at	No. of Wheels	VEHICLE. Class.		WORKING. From	WORKING. To	RETURNING BY TRAIN. Time.	RETURNING BY TRAIN. From
1903	5 10 p.m. (Mail)	Penzance ...	4.5 a.m.		Bk. Van	X	North Rd.	Paddington	9. 5 p.m.	Paddingt'n
					P.O. Carr. 830-1 or 2	X	,,	,,	,,	,,
					P.O. Carr. 847-8 or 9	X	,,	,,	,,	,,
					P.O. Carr. 834-5 or 6	X	Penzance	,,	,,	,,
					P.O. Carr. 851-2 or 3	X	,,	,,	,,	,,
					Bk. Van 1063-4 or 5		,,	,,	,,	,,
					Bk. Compo ...	X	,,	,,	1.45 p.m.	,,
					Van	X	Exeter ...	,,	9. 5 p.m.	,,
1905 and 1919	p.m. 6 0 (Mail) *	Penzance	a.m. 3 50		Brake Van...		Penzance ...	Paddington	p.m. 9 5	Paddington
					Parcel Post Sorting Van		,,	,,	,,	,,
					Mail Tender		,,	,,	,,	,,
					Letter Car ...		,,	,,	,,	,,
					Cape Mail Coach ...		,,	,,	,,	,,
					Stowing Van		,,	,,	,,	,,
					Brake Van...		,,	,,	,,	,,
					P'rc'l P'st V'n		Exeter ...	,,	,,	,,
1929	6 48 p.m. (Mail) Penzance due 3 50 a.m. *			70	Siphon G		Kingswear ...	Paddington	1.40 a.m. ..	Paddington
					Bk. Van......		Penzance	,,	10.10 p.m. ..	,,
					P.O Carr..... 830–1 or 2		,,	,,	,,	,,
					P.O. Carr..... 847–8 or 9		,,	,,	,,	,,
					P.O. Carr. ... 834–5 or 6		,,	,,	,,	,,
					P.O. Carr. ... 850–2 or 3		,,	,,	,,	,,
					Bk. Van...... 1063–4 or 5		,,	,,	,,	,,
					Siphon G		Exeter	,,	,,	,,

TABLE 1 — 10.00 p.m. PADDINGTON – PENZANCE
Great Western TPO (Sundays)

YEAR	Train.	From Paddington To	VEHICLE.		WORKING. From	WORKING. To		RETURNING BY		Due at Paddington at	
1903	9 5 p.m. (Mail) *	Plym'th 70′ (North Rd.) due 4.7 a.m.	Bk. Van 1063-4 or 5	XF	Padd'ton	Penzance		5.10 p.m.	Penzance	4. 5 a.m.	
		70′	P.O. Carr. 851-2 or 3	XF	,,	,,		,,	,,	,,	
		(*Saturdays excepted*)	P.O. Carr. 834-5 or 6	XF	,,	,,		,,	,,	,,	
			P.O. Carr. 847-8 or 9	X	,,	Plymouth (North Rd.)		8.30 p.m.	Plymouth (North Rd.)	,,	
			P.O. Carr. 830-1 or 2	X	,,	,,		,,	,,	,,	
			Brake Van ...	X	,,	,,		,,	,,	,,	
			Van 876 or 7	X	,,	Exeter		10.11 p.m.	Exeter ...	,,	
	10 0 p.m.	Pen-zance due 7.55 a.m. 70′	Brake Van ... 1063-4 or 5	X E	North Rd.	Penzance ..		5.10 p.m.	Penzance	4. 5 a.m.	
			P. O. Carr. 851-2 or 3	X E	,,	,,		,,	,,	,,	
			P. O. Carr. 834-5 or 6	X E	,,	,,		,,	,,	,,	
		70′	Van	X	Paddington	,,		,,	,,	3.15 a.m.	J
			Third	X	,,	,,		,,	,,	,,	
			SleepingCar	X	,,	,,		12. 5 a.m.	Plymouth	6.45 a.m.	
			Compo	X N	,,	,,		5.10 p.m.	Penzance	3.15 a.m.	J
			V'n 3rd(3c)	X Q	,,	,,		,,	,,	,,	
			Van Third	X	,,	Plymouth	G	4. 0 p.m.	Plymouth	2.45 a.m.	MO
			Third	X	,,	,,	G	,,	,,	,,	MO
			Compo	X	,,	,,	G	,,	,,	,,	MO
			Van Third	X	,,	,,	G	,,	,,	,,	MO

E Off 9.5 p.m. Paddington.
F On from Plymouth by 10.0 p.m. Paddington.
G These Vehicles are detached at North Road and work thence to Millbay at 5.0 a.m.
J Saturday's Train, on from Plymouth 9.0 p.m. thence.
N Three First and four Third Class Compartments.
Q Open Vehicle, *i.e.*, without partition in Guard's Compartment.
R Due Gloucester 12.10 a.m.
T Runs to Neyland if no passengers for Pembroke Dk.

TABLE 2

BRISTOL – PENZANCE TPO
BRISTOL – PLYMOUTH TPO

Timings 1908 See previous table.

Coach Allocations

Date	*Coach No.*	*Nets*	*Arms*
1903	838 (2080) 840 (2084) 841 (2086)	1ns	4ns
1913	838, 840, 841	1ns	6ns
1920	838 840, 862, 864, 865	1ns 1ns	6ns 4ns
1926	840 842, 845, 838	1ns/1os 1ns	6ns/2os 4ns
1935	799, 800	1ns	4ns
1951	797, 799, 800	1ns	4ns
1963	799, 800	1ns	4ns

As from 26th March 1930 service ran to Plymouth.
Service ceased 3rd March 1972.

TABLE 1 & 2

1. GREAT WESTERN T.P.O.
2. BRISTOL – PENZANCE T.P.O.

Station	*1907 GREAT WESTERN T.P.O. Down* P.M.			*Up* A.M.			*1908 BRISTOL–PENZANCE T.P.O. Down*			*Up*		
PADDINGTON	9.05			3.50								
Southall	9.18	1	3	3.38	4	0						
West Drayton	9.23	3	4	3.35	1	2						
Slough	9.30	3	3	3.27	3	3						
Maidenhead	9.37	1	3	3.20	3	2						
READING	9.53 9.59			3.05 3.00								
DIDCOT	10.23 10.28			2.37 2.33								
STEVENTON				2.26 2.24								
Wantage Road	10.39	2	1									
SWINDON	11.01 11.07			1.57 1.52								
CHIPPENHAM	11.30 11.34			1.29 1.25								
BATH	11.54 12.00			1.05 1.00								
BRISTOL	12.18 12.30			12.43 12.32			A.M. 6.15			P.M. 7.12		
Flax Bourton							6.28	1	0			
Nailsea							6.31	1	0			
Yatton	12.49	3	5	12.17	1	3	6.36	4	1	6.58	1	3
Hewish							6.38	1	1			
Weston-S-Mare	12.56			12.07	2	5a	6.42	MO		6.52	1	1
Highbridge							6.53	2	2	6.42	2	2
BRIDGWATER	1.13 1.17			11.48 11.44			7.06	2	2	6.35	1	1
TAUNTON	1.33 1.39			11.28 11.23			7.34 7.41			6.20 6.12		
Wellington							7.53	1	1	6.00	1	1
Tiverton Junc.	2.04	4	0	11.01	1	5				5.49	1	1
Cullompton	2.09	4	1	10.57	1	4	8.15	1	1	5.45	1	1
EXETER	2.24 2.31			10.40 10.29			8.30 8.37			5.30 5.22		
Dawlish	2.48	2	0	10.13	0	3	8.53					
Teignmouth	2.54	4	0	10.07	1	2	8.57					
NEWTON ABBOT	3.02 3.09			9.58 9.50			9.05			4.53 4.42		
Langford Bridge							9.07					
Totnes	3.24	5	5	9.36	3	3	9.18			4.27	1	1
Brent	3.37	5	0	9.26	0	4	9.31					
Ivybridge	3.44	2	2	9.19	2	2	9.38			4.10		
Plympton	3.52	1	1	9.07	2	2	9.48			3.57		
PLYMOUTH	4.00 4.10			9.00 8.48			9.54 10.00			3.50 3.40		
DEVONPORT							10.07			3.36 3.37		
SALTASH	4.20 4.22			8.38 8.36						3.24		
St. Germans	4.31	2	1	8.27	1	1	10.22					
LISKEARD							10.39 10.37			2.56 2.54		
BODMIN RD.	5.00 5.03			7.54 7.52			10.57 10.59			2.34 2.33		
Lostwithiel	5.09	2	2	7.45	1	1	11.04			2.24		
PAR	5.16 5.19			7.36 7.33			11.11			2.12		
St. Austell	5.29	5	1	7.26	1	5	11.23			2.02		
Grampound Road	5.40	3	1	7.10	1	3	11.34			1.44		
TRURO	5.53 5.58			7.00 6.55			11.47 11.51			1.28 1.20		
Chacewater							12.03			1.10		
Scorrier	6.10	2	1	6.43	2	3	12.09			1.01		
Redruth	6.15	5	3	6.39	1	3	12.16			12.55		
Carn Brea							12.21			12.47		
Camborne	6.20	3	1	6.32	1	3	12.37			12.42		
GWINEAR ROAD				6.27 6.25			12.33			12.34		
Hayle							12.40			12.22		
ST. ERTH	6.32 6.34			6.13 6.11						12.16		
Marazion Rd.	6.41	2	1	6.08	1	2	12.55			12.06		
PENZANCE	6.45 (A.M.)			6.00 (P.M.)			1.00 (A.M.)			12.00 Noon		

MO Monday only – stop
a Number of bags varied

Times given for passing apparatus point, not station.

TABLE 2	BRISTOL – PENZANCE TPO									
YEAR	Train.	From	To	VEHICLE. Owning Co.	VEHICLE. Class.	WORKING. From	WORKING. To	RETURNING BY Time	RETURNING BY From	
1903 DOWN	1 25 a.m. (Mail)	Crewe ...	Penzance E due 1.30 p.m.	G.W.	Mail Van ...	Bristol	North-Rd. U	12.0 noon	Penzance	
				G.W.	Van Third X	B Shrewsb'y	Penzance E	11.20 a.m.	Plymouth	P
				N.W.	Bk. Van ... X	Liverpool...	,, E	2.30 p.m	,,	P
				G.W.	Bk. Compo(2) X	,,	,, E	,,	,,	
				G.W.	Bk. Compo(2) X	M'chester	,, E	,,	,,	T
				G.W.	Third X	,,	,, E	,,	,,	
				N.W.	Bk. Van ... X	,,	,, E	4. 5 p.m.	Penzance	
				G.W.	Compo ... X	,,	,,	,,	,,	
				N.W.	Bk Van ... X	,,	Plymouth	2.30 p.m.	Plymouth	
				W.C.J.S.	Bk.Compo X	A Glasgow	,,	,,	,,	
				—	6-w.Fish Van	Aberdeen	Bristol	—	—	
1905 DOWN	a.m. 2 20 (Mail)	Shrewsb'y	Penzance	G.W.	Van F ...	Bristol ...	Exeter E	10.40 a.m.	Plymouth	
				G.W.	Mail Van ...	,,	Penzance	12. 0 noon	Penzance	
				G.W.	Third ...	,,	,,	—	—	J
				N.W.	Bk. Van ...	Liverpool	P'nzance A	2.27 ,,	Bristol	R
				N.W.	Tri-Compo	,,	,, A	,,	,,	R
				N.W.	Bk. Van ...	M'chester	,,	4.45 ,,	Penzance	
				G.W.	Bk.Tri-Comp	Plymouth	Penzance	,,	,,	
				G.W.	Tri-Compo	M'chester	Plym'th U	2.27 p.m.	Plym'th	R
				N.W	Bk. Van ...	,,	,, U	,,	,,	R
				—	Fish Van ...	Grimsby	,,	—	—	
				W.C.J.	Bk. End Sleeping Compo(1 & 3)	Glasgow D	Exeter	2.27 p.m.	Plymouth	
				—	Fish Van ...	Aberdeen	,,	—	—	
				—	Fish Van ..	Leeds	,,	—	—	
				G.W.	6-wh.Parcels Van	Birm'ng'm	,,	8.30 a.m.	Bristol	B

A On Sunday mornings runs to Plymouth only.
B Via Didcot.
C Arrives Shrewsbury 11.58 p.m,
D Has two First Class Compartments, in one of which two beds are made up.
E From Exeter to Newton Abbot at 8.51 a.m.
F Wingless Van.

J See note C, page 10.
R Penzance to Plymouth at 6.15 p.m.
U Plymouth to Penzance at 11.12 a.m.

TABLE 2	BRISTOL – PENZANCE TPO							
YEAR	Train.	VEHICLE. Owning Co.	VEHICLE. Class.	WORKING. From	WORKING. To	BALANCE. Time	BALANCE. From	
1929 DOWN	*1 25 a.m. Crewe to Penzance (Mondays only) due 1.30 p.m.* *	*G.W.*	*Mail Van No. 838 or 840*	*Bristol ....*	*North Road.*	*3.55 p.m.*	*North Road*	*Mons.*
		G.W.	*Third .... +*	,,	,,	—	—	
		G.W.	*Third .... +*	,,	*Penzance ..*	—	—	
		G.W.	*Third .... +*	,,	,,	—	—	
		G.W.	*Compo ...... +*	,,	,,	—	—	
		L M S	*Van Third ..*	*Manchester .*	,,	*4.30 p.m. ..*	*Penzance ..*	} *Mons*
		L M S	*Compo ....*	,,	,,	,,	,,	
		L M S	*Bk. Van ...*	,,	,,	,,	,,	
		L M S	*Bk. Van ...*	*Manchester .*	*Cardiff.....*	*12. 5 a.m. ..*	*Cardiff.....*	*Tues*
		G.W.	*Compo ....*	,,	,,	*2.15 p.m. ..*	,,	} *Mons*
		G.W.	*Van Third ..*	,,	,,	,,	,,	
		G.W.	*Compo ......*	*Liverpool ..*	,,	*12. 5 a.m. ..*	,,	} *Tues.*
		G.W.	*Van Third ..*	,,	,,	,,	,,	
		G.W.	*Bk. Compo ..*	,,	,,	*12.40 p.m. ..*	,,	*Suns.*
		G.W.	*Compo ......*	,,	,,	*12.30 p.m. ..*	,,	} *Mons.*
		G.W.	*Van Third ...*	,,	,,	,,	,,	N
DOWN	2 40 a.m. (Mail) Shrewsbury to Penzance (*Tuesdays to Saturdays*) due 1.30 p.m. *	G.W.	Mail Van No. 838 or 840	Bristol	North Road.	3 55 p.m. ..	North Road	
		G.W.	Bk. Compo .. B	Glasgow ...	Penzance .. } F	12.10 p.m. ..	Penzance ..	
		L M S	Van Third....	Liverpool ..	,,	4.30 p.m. ..	,,	
		L M S	Compo	,,	,,	,,	,,	
		L M S	Bk. Van......	,,	,,	,,	,,	
		L M S	Van Third....	Manchester.	,, } F	,,	,,	
		L M S	Compo	,,	,,	,,	,,	
		L M S	Bk. Van......	,,	,,	,,	,,	
		G.W.	Bk. Van......	,,	Kingswear .	5.40 p.m. ..	Kingswear .	
		G.W.	Bk. Compo...	Birkenhead	Bristol C	9.45 a.m. ..	Bristol	

C Attached at Shrewsbury off 11.20 p.m. ex Birkenhead.
D Works 5.25 p.m. Cardiff to Bristol, 11.25 p.m. Bristol to Plymouth.
E Detached at Shrewsbury for 2.40 a.m. thence.

F Off 1.25 a.m. ex Crewe.
N To Manchester.

The return working is covered in TABLE 5
CARDIFF – CREWE TPO
12.10 Penzance to Crewe (Plymouth – Bristol)

TABLE 2	PENZANCE – BRISTOL TPO									
YEAR	Train.	To Paddington From	Due at Paddington at		VEHICLE.	WORKING. From	WORKING. To	RETURNING BY		
1903 UP	12 0 noon	Penzance ...	10.30 p.m.		Van Third X	Kingswear	Paddington	1.45 p.m.	Paddingt'n	
					Compo X	,,	,,	,,	,,	
					Mail Van ...	North Road	Bristol	6.20 a.m.	Bristol	
					Van Thd(3) X	Penzance ...	Paddington	5.30 a.m.	Paddingt'n	
					Compo (4) X	,,	,,	,,	,,	
					Third X	,,	,,	,,	,,	
					Third X	,,	,,	,,	,,	
					Van Thd (3) X	,,	,,	,,	,,	
					Milk Truck S	X ,,	Bristol ... C	For Mid.	Line.	
					Milk Truck ...	Penryn	North Road	3.35 p.m.	Newton A.	
					Van	Yeovil	Newcastle E	10. 0 p.m.	York	
1905 UP	noon. 12 0 (Mail)	Penzance ...	10.10 p.m.		Mail Van ...	Penzance ...	Bristol	6.15 a.m.	Bristol	
					Bk.Third(3c)	,,	Paddington	12.25 p.m.	Paddington	} CT
					Compo	,,	,,	,,	,,	
					Third	,,	,,	,,	,,	
					Bk.Third(3c)	,,	,,	,,	,,	
					Bk.Tri- Com.	,,	,,	,,	,,	
					Compo (Corr)	Kingswear	,,	9.0 a.m.	,,	
					Bk.Third(4c)	,,	,,	,,	,,	
					Milk Truck	S *Penzance*	~~Bristol~~	—	—	
					Milk Truck	S ,,	,,	—	—	
					6-wh Van L	Bristol ...	Sheffield......	—	—	

C From Southampton at 5.28 p.m.

L Detached at Swindon for 8.45 p.m. via Banbury. G.W. and G.C. Vehicle alternate days.
T Through to Paddington on Saturdays.

YEAR	Train.	To Paddington From	Due at Paddington at		VEHICLE.	WORKING. From	WORKING. To	RETURNING BY		
1919 UP	noon. 12 0 (Mail)	Penzance ...	p.m. 10 10	8	Mail Van ...	Penzance ...	Bristol	a.m. 6 15	Bristol	
				8	Van............	,,	Paddington	9 0	Paddington	} H
				8	Compo	,,	,,	,,	,,	
				8	Third	,,	,,	,,	,,	
				8	Bk.Third(4c)	,,	,,	,,	,,	
				8	Bk.Third(4c)	Kingswear	,,	,,	,,	
				8	Compo	,,	,,	,,	,,	
				8	Bk.Third(4c)	,,	,,	,,	,,	
				6	*Milk Truck*	S *Penzance*	*Bristol*	—	—	
				6	*Milk Truck*	S ,,	,,	p.m.	—	
				8	Bk. Tri-Com	,,	Newton......	6 30	L ,,	
				6	Van............	Bristol ...	Sheffield K	—	—	

H Fitted with Electrical Communication.

K Detached at Swindon for 8.45 p.m. thence via Banbury. G.W. and G.C. Vehicle alternate days.
L To Plymouth, returning to Newton Abbot by 8.30 a.m. ex Plymouth.

YEAR	Train.	From	To		Owning Co.	Class	Working From	Working To	Returning Time	Returning From
1919 DOWN	a.m. 2 20 (Mail)	Shrewsb'y	Penzance	8	G.W.	Mail Van ...	Bristol ...	Penzance	noon 12 0	Penzance
				8	G.W.	Third ...	,,	,,	p.m. 4 45	,,
				8	G.W.	Bk. Van ...	Liverpool	,, } A	7 40	Bristol R
				8	N.W.	Tri-Compo	,,	,,	,,	,, R
				8	G.W.	Bk. Van ...	M'chester	P'nzance A	4 45	Penzance
				8	G.W.	Tri-Compo	,,	,, A	7 40	Bristol R
				8	N.W.	Bk. Van ...	,,	Plym'th E	,,	,,
				—	—	Fish Van ...	Grimsby	,,	—	—
				8	W.C.J.	Bk. End Com (1 & 3)	Glasgow	,,	7 40	Bristol
				—	—	Fish Van ...	Aberdeen	Bristol	—	—
				—	—	Fish Van ...	Leeds	,,	—	—
				6	G.W.	Parcels Van	Birm'ng'm	,,	a.m 8 30	Bristol B

TABLE 3 — 5.30 a.m. PADDINGTON – PENZANCE

YEAR	Train.	From Paddington To	VEHICLE.	WORKING. From	WORKING. To	RETURNING BY		Due at Paddington at
1903	5 30 a.m. (Mail)	Penzance ... due 4.35 p.m.	Siphon G ... X	Paddington	Taunton C	4. 0 p.m.	Plymouth	2.45 a.m.
			Letter Car ...	,,	Bristol ...	11.30 a.m.	Bristol ...	3. 0 p.m.
			Van X	,,	Plymouth ...	4. 0 p.m.	Plymouth	2.45 a.m.
			Compo ...... X MO	,,	,,	—	—	—
			Van 3rd(3c) X N	,,	Penzance ...	12. 0noon	Penzance	10.30 p.m.
			Third X	,,	,,	,,	,,	,,
			Third X	,,	,,	,,	,,	,,
		70′	Compo (4) X	,,	,,	,,	,,	,,
			Van 3rd (3c) X N	,,	,,	,,	,,	,,
			Siphon G ... X	,,	Plymouth ...	12. 5 a.m.	Plymouth	6.45 a.m.
			News Van ...	,,	Kingswear W	6.55 p.m.	T'stock Jc.	2.15 a.m.
			News Van ... J	,,	Carmarthen	3. 0 p.m.	Neyland ...	4. 5 a.m.
			News Van ...	,,	Cheltenh'm G	12.47 a.m.	Gloucester	,,
			News Van ...	,,	Banbury ...	1.17 p.m.	Banbury ...	2.45 p.m.
			Bk. Van	,,	,,	7.15 p.m.	,,	To S. Lambeth

C On Mondays detached at Bristol and thence 9.30 a.m. Bristol to Taunton; 2.30 p.m. Taunton to Exeter; 4.20 p.m. Exeter to Taunton.

G 7.40 a.m. Swindon to Cheltenham.

J Via Swindon and on by 7.30 a.m. to Cardiff, thence 12.20 p.m. to Neyland.

N These must be open Van Thirds, *i.e.*, without partition in Guards' portion.

W 6.25. p.m. Kingswear to Newton Abbot.

YEAR	Train.	From Paddington To	VEHICLE.	WORKING. From	WORKING. To	RETURNING BY		Due at Paddington at
1905	a.m. 5 30 (Mail) •	Penzance ...	Letter Car ...	Paddington	Bristol	3. 2 p.m.	Bristol	6. 0 p.m.
			Third ... MO	*Swindon* ...	*Plymouth* ...	—	—	—
			Third ... MO	,,	,,	—	—	—
			Compo	Paddington	Plymouth...	10.40 a.m.	Plymouth	6. 0 p.m.
			Van.....	,,	Penzance ...	1.40 ,,	Penzance ...	2.50 a.m.
			Bk.Third(4c)	,,	,,	10.15 ,,	Weymouth B	3.10 p.m.
			Compo	,,	,,	,,	,, B	,,
			Bk.Third(4c)	,,	,,	,,	,, B	,,
			News Van C	,,	Paignton ...	1.40 p.m.	Penzance	2 50 a.m.
			News Van D	,,	*Bristol*	*10. 5* a.m.	*Bristol*	*1.20* p.m.
			News Van ... J	,,	New Milford	10.40 p.m.	Cardiff E	3.30 a.m.
			Van......MO	*CliftonDown*	*Paignton* ..	—	—	—
			Third	Truro.........	Penzance ...	8.45 p.m.	Penzance ...	—

B 6.15 p.m. Penzance to Plymouth; 6.25 a.m. Plymouth to Taunton; 11.17 a.m. Taunton to Bristol; 5.0 p.m. Bristol to Westbury and Chippenham; 8.20 p.m. Chippenham to Weymouth.
C Locally Paignton to North Road.
D Thursdays, Fridays and Saturdays only.
E Locally New Milford to Cardiff.
J Via Bath.

YEAR	Train.	From Paddington To	VEHICLE.	WORKING. From	WORKING. To	RETURNING BY		Due at Paddington at
1919	a.m. 5 30 (Mail) •	Falmouth ...	Letter Car ...	Paddington	Bristol	p.m. 3 0	Bristol	p.m. 6 0
			Van.....	Paddington	Plymouth A	p.m. 1 40	Penzance	a.m. 2 50
			Third ... MO	*Swindon* ...	,,	—	—	—
			Bk.Tri-Cmpo	Paddington	Truro F	4 45	Penzance ...	3 30
			Bk.Third(4c)	,,	Falmouth ...	a.m. 10 15	Weymouth B	p.m. 3 10
			Compo	,,	,,	,,	,, B	,,
			Third	,,	,,	,,	,, B	,,
			Van...........	,,	,,	,,	,, B	,,
			News Van C	,,	Kingswear	p.m. 1 40	Penzance	a.m. 2 50
			News Van D	,,	*Bristol*	*5 52*	*Bristol*	p.m. *8 30*
			News Van ...	,,	New Milford via Bath	10 40	Cardiff E	a.m. 3 30

A Plymouth to Penzance 9.25 a.m.
B 3.25 p.m. Falmouth to Plymouth; 6.25 a.m. Plymouth to Taunton; 11.17 a.m. Taunton to Bath; 3.31 p.m. Bath to Chippenham; 8.20 p.m. Chippenham to Weymouth.
C Off at Exeter; on by 6.55 a.m. Bristol. Locally Kingswear to North Road.
D Thursdays Fridays and Saturdays only.
E Locally New Milford to Cardiff.

F Truro to Penzance on 6.55 a.m. ex Bristol.

TABLE 3
BRISTOL SORTING CARRIAGE
(5.30 a.m. Paddington – Penzance)

TIMINGS (Apparatus working)

Station	1924 Down		1924 Up		1929 Down	1929 Up	
PADDINGTON	5.30		6.00		5.30	11.30	
Southall	5.43	2 0	–			↑ Carriage returns light from Bristol	1929 Down
Hayes	5.46	2 1a	–				Reading 6.18
West Drayton	5.48	3 2b	5.42	1 1			Swindon 7.24
Slough	5.53	1 0	–				Bath 8.10
Maidenhead	6.00	3 2b	5.20	1 5			
Cholsey	6.34	1 0	4.53	1 2			
Chippenham	–		3.42	2 2			
Corsham	–		3.37	1 0			
BRISTOL	8.28		3.00		8.51	9.15	

1903 timings – See 1898 Timetable.

a. TTHSO.
b. SO.
Southall suspended 31.1.20.

COACH ALLOCATIONS

1903 Roster	Nos. 842, 845	Net 1 ns	Arms 4 ns	
1920 Roster	No. 838	Net 1 ns	Arms 6 ns	No nets or arms on the off side of the vehicles
	No. 840	Net 1 ns	Arms 4 ns	
1926 Roster	Nos. 842, 845	Net 1 ns	Arms 4 ns	
1935 Roster	Nos. 798, 800	Net 1 ns	Arms 4 ns	

Service ceased 21st September 1940

TABLE 3 — 5.30 a.m. PADDINGTON – PENZANCE

YEAR	Train from Paddington.		VEHICLE.		WORKING From	WORKING To		BALANCE;		Due at Paddington at	
1929	5 30 a.m. (Mail) to Penzance due 3 43 p.m.		Third........	+MX	Swindon ..	Bristol		10.52 a.m.	Bristol to Swindon	11.30 a.m.	MX
			Letter Car ... 842 or 845		Paddington	,,		9.15 a.m.	,,		
			Third........	MO	*Swindon* ...	*North Road*		—	—	—	
			Compo.......	MO	,,	,,		—	—	—	
			Van	MX	Sheffield ...	Kingsbridge	N	12.10 p.m.	Penzance to Sheffield		SX
			Van..........	*RR*	,,	*Helston*	N	,,	,,	,,	*RR*
			Bk. Van......	MX	,,	Penzance ..	R	,,	,,	,,	SX
			Bk. Van......	MX	Birmingham	,,	Y	12.55 p.m.	,, to Birmingham		SX KK
			Bk. Van......	MX	Leeds .... (Wellington)	,,	AA	12.10 p.m.	,, to Leeds		SX
			Stores Van ...	+TO	*Paddington* .	,,		—	—	—	
		70	Van Third....	B	,,	,,	P				
		70	Third........		,,	,,	P	1.25 p.m.	Taunton ...	6.15 p.m.	TX
		70	Compo		,,	,,	P	*11.35 a.m.*	*Penzance* ..	*7.55 p.m.*	*Suns.*
		70	Van Third....	A	,,	,,	P			,,	
			Van		,,	Plymouth ..		4.20 p.m.	Plymouth ..	2.40 a.m.	
			Siphon G		,,	,,		6.20 p.m.	,,	,,	GG
			News Bk. Van		,,	Kingswear .		8.43 p.m.	Taunton ...	,,	M
			Siphon G		,,	Taunton ...	C	7.50 p.m.	,,	,,	BB
			Siphon G.....		,,	Carmarthen	J	5.17 p.m.	Carmarthen	2.25 a.m.	L
			News Van ...		,,	Cheltenham	D	8.50 p.m.	Swindon ...	10.25 p.m.	CC
			News Van ...		,,	Banbury ...		10.42 a.m.	Banbury ...	2.38 p.m.	
			Bk. Van......	+	,,	Worcester..		6.47 a.m.	Worcester ..	12.20 a.m.	K
			News Van....		,,	Chippenham	G	7.55 p.m.	Chippenham	12. 0 night	

C 11.55 a.m. Taunton to Wellington **SX**; 7.0 p.m. thence to Taunton **SX**

D Detached at Swindon and forward by 7.43 a.m. thence.

G Detached at Reading and forward by 6.50 a.m. thence to Chippenham.

J To Bristol and on by 7.40 a.m. Bridgwater to Carmarthen

K 6.52 a.m. Didcot to Oxford; 7.32 a.m. Oxford to Worcester.

L From Carmarthen Jc. by 2.25 p.m. ex Neyland **SX**; and 12.0 noon ex Neyland **SO**.

M 2.20 p.m. Kingswear to Exeter. Next day 7.35 a.m.. Exeter to Tiverton Junction; 6-35 p.m. Tiverton Junction to Taunton.

N Attached at Bristol off 10.13 p.m. ex York

P 7.5 p.m. Penzance to North Road **SX**; 9.20 p.m. Plymouth to Newton Abbot **MX**; 6.20 a.m. Newton Abbot to Kingswear **TX**; 8.10 a.m. Kingswear to Exeter **TX**; 11.0 a.m. Exeter to Taunton **TX**.

R Attached at Bristol off 10.13 p.m. York. (Vans, Nos 221, 1054 and 1055, allotted to this service.)

AA Attached at Bristol off 10.0 p.m. ex Leeds.

BB 7.50 p.m. Taunton to Bristol; 11.15 p.m. thence.

CC 10.43 a.m. Cheltenham to Gloucester; 7.5 p.m. thence to Swindon.

GG Return by 7.0 a.m. ex Plymouth, Sundays.

KK 6.35 p.m. Taunton to Birmingham.

YEAR	Train.	To Paddington From	Due at Paddington at	VEHICLE.	WORKING. From	WORKING. To	RETURNING BY		
1903	11 30 a.m.	Bristol ...... (via Devizes)	3. 0 p.m.	Third	Reading ...	Paddington	Balanced locally		
				Compo	,,	,,	Balanced locally		
				Bk. Compo ...	,,	,,	Balanced locally		
				Letter Car ...	Bristol	,,	5.30 a.m.	Paddingt'n	
				Compo X	,,	,,	6.30 p.m.	,,	
				Van Third ...	,,	,,	12. 5 a.m.	,,	L
				Compo	,,	,,	,,	,,	L
				Compo	,,	,,	,,	,,	L
				Van Third ...	,,	,,	,,	,,	
1919	a.m. 10 40 (Mail)	Plymouth...	6. 0 p.m.	6-wh. News Van	Newton Abbot	Bristol	6.15 a.m.	Bristol	
				Bk. Compo 1 & 3 (Mid)	Kingswear	Bradford	1.10 p.m.	Paddington	
				Letter Car	Bristol	Paddington	5.30 a.m.	,,	
				6-wh. Van A	*Plymouth* ...	,,	*1*B*10* p.m.	,,	
				Parcels Van	,,	,,	12.0 night	,,	
				Third	,,	,,	C11.40a.m	,,	
				Compo	,,	,,	5.30 a.m.	,,	
				Compo	,,	,,	11.40 a.m.	,,	
				Third	,,	,,	3.3 p.m.	,,	
				Bk.Third(4c)	,,	,,	7.30 a.m.	,,	

A Wednesdays and Saturdays only. For Hotel and Refreshment Room Stores.
B Tuesdays and Fridays only.
C 11.40 a.m. Paddington to Cardiff, 6.43 p.m. Cardiff to Swansea, 1.50 p.m. Swansea to Swindon, 7.27 a.m. Swindon to Bristol, 6.15 a.m. Bristol to Penzance, and 6.15 p.m. Penzance to Plymouth

TABLE 4
BRISTOL – EXETER TPO
(9.00 a.m. Paddington – Penzance)

TIMINGS 1908

		P.M.		
BRISTOL		12.07	↑	*(10.00 – 1908 duty book)*
Yatton	A	12.27		
Weston-S-Mare	A	12.34		
Highbridge	A	12.43		
Bridgwater	A	12.50	— Carriage returns empty —	
TAUNTON arr.		1.05		
dept.		1.10		
Wellington	A	1.18		
Tiverton Junc.	A	1.30		
Cullompton	A	1.34		
EXETER		1.52	7.48	*(6.49 – 1908 duty book)*

In the down direction the train continued on to Penzance.

COACH ALLOCATIONS

1903 Roster Nos. 839 (2083) Net 1 ns, Arms 4 ns.
1915 Roster Nos. 839
Spares 838, 840, 841, 862

Service ceased as a TPO March 1917*

*The coach was still working through to Exeter in 1919 (May) but had ceased by 1920 when No. 839 was a spare at Henley-on-Thames.

TABLE 4 PADDINGTON – PENZANCE

YEAR	Train.	From Paddington To	VEHICLE. Class.	WORKING. From	WORKING. To	RETURNING BY TRAIN. Time.	RETURNING BY TRAIN. From	Due at Paddn. at	
1903	9 0 a.m. (Mail) *	Bristol due 12.2 p.m.	Van Third X	Paddington	Bristol … } K	8.48 a.m.	Weston-s. Mare	12.40 p.m.	
			Compo ……X	,,	,, } K	,,	,,	,,	
			Compo (4) X	,,	,, } K	,,	,,	,,	
			Compo (4) X	,,	,, } K	,,	,,	,,	
			Third (10c) X	,,	,, } K	,,	,,	,,	
			Van Third X	,,	,, } K	,,	,,	,,	
			Siphon G …X	,,	,,	8. 0 a.m.	Exeter …	3.25 p.m.	
			Third ……X MO	,,	Bristol ……	—	—	—	
			Ref. Van … Y	,,	,,	*1.15 p.m.*	*Taunton* …	*6.10 p.m.*	WO

K 12.40 p.m. (S.O.) 5.15 p.m. (SX) Bristol to Weston.

Y Tuesdays only: 3.15 p.m. Bristol to Plymouth; 9.20 a.m. Plymouth to Exeter, 12.17 p.m. Exeter to Taunton Wednesdays.

YEAR	Train.	From Paddington To	VEHICLE. Class.	WORKING. From	WORKING. To	RETURNING BY TRAIN. Time.	RETURNING BY TRAIN. From	Due at Paddn. at	
1905	a.m. 9 0 (Mail) *	Penzance ..	Bk.Third(5c)	Paddington	Carmarthen	8.20 a.m.	Carmarthen	10. 0 p.m.	
			Compo ……	,,	,,	,,	,,	,, L	
			Bk.Third(4c)	,,	,,	,,	,,	,, L	
			Third MO	,,	,,	—	—	—	
			Mail Coach	Bristol ……	Exeter .. …	7.48 p.m.	Exeter	—	
			Bk.Third(4c)	Paddington	Kingswear	3.50 ,,	Kingswear	10.10 p.m.	
			Compo(Corr).	,,	,,	,,	,,	,,	
			Bk.Third(4c)	,,	Penzance …	9.10 a.m.	Falmouth …	6.40 ,,	} O
			Compo ……	,,	,,	,,	,,	,,	} O
			Third ………	,,	,,	,,	,,	,,	} O
			Van …………	,,	,,	,,	,,	,,	} O
			Bk.Tri-Cmpo	N'wt'n Ab'ot	,,	2. 0 p.m.	Penzance …	—	
			News Van S	,,	*North Road*	*1.40* ,,	,,	*2.50* a.m.	
			Bk.Third N	*Plymouth* …	*Truro* ……	7.46 a.m.	Truro …	—	
			Bk.Third SO	,,	,,	6.7 p.m.	,,	—	
			Compo F	Truro ……	Penzance …	10.35 a.m.	Penzance …	—	
			Bk. Third F	,,	,,	,,	,, H	—	
		(Slip)	Tri-Compo…	Didcot ……	Wantage Rd	—	—	SCW 1	
		(Slip)	Tri-Compo…	Swindon …	Frome K	—	—	SCW 2	
			Bk. Third …	,,	,, K	1.55 p.m.	Frome …	—	
		(Slip)	Tri-Compo…	Bristol ……	Bridgwater	—	—	SCW 13	

F To Truro on 3.58 p.m. ex North Road.
H Locally Birkenhead to Shrewsbury.

N Mondays, Tuesdays, Thursdays and Saturdays.
O 8.0 a.m. Penzance to Plymouth, 3.58 p.m. North Road to Falmouth.
Q Slipped at Patney & Chirton.
R Slipped at Newbury.
W Arriving at Exeter by 6.55 a.m. Bristol.
X To Manchester.

YEAR	Train.	From Paddington To	VEHICLE. Class.	WORKING. From	WORKING. To	RETURNING BY TRAIN. Time.	RETURNING BY TRAIN. From	Due at Paddn. at	
1919	a.m. 9 0 (Mail) *	Penzance …	Mail Coach	Bristol ……	Exeter .. …	p.m. 7 48	Exeter	p.m. —	
			Bk.Third(4c)	Paddington	Kingswear	3 50	Kingswear	10 10	} J
			Compo ……	,,	,,	,,	,,	,,	} J
			Bk.Third(4c)	,,	,,	,,	,,	,,	} J
			Bk.Third(4c)	,,	Penzance …	noon 12 0	Penzance	,,	} J
			Compo ……	,,	,,	,,	,,	,,	} J
			Third ………	,,	,,	,,	,,	,,	} J
			Van …………	,,	,,	,,	,,	,,	} J
			Bk.Third MO	*Paddington*	*Cardiff* ……	—	—	—	
			Bk.Tri-Cmpo	Newton……	Penzance …	12 0	Penzance …	—	
			News Van S	,,	North Road	p.m. 1 40	,,	a.m. 2 50	
		(Slip)	Tri-Compo…	Didcot ……	Wantage Rd	—	SCW 1	—	
		(Slip)	Tri-Compo…	Swindon …	Frome K	—	SCW 2	—	
			Van…………	,,	,, K	1 55	Frome ……	—	
		(Slip)	Tri-Compo…	Bristol ……	Bridgwater	—	SCW 3	—	
			Bk.Third L	Plymouth …	Truro ..	a.m. 7 46	Truro	—	
			Third … SO	,,	,,	4 50	Penzance }	Sun-days	
			Bk. Third SO	,,	,,	,,	,, }		

J Fitted with Electrical communication.
K Slipped at Chippenham.
L Mondays, Tuesdays, Thursdays, and Saturdays.

TABLE 5

CARDIFF – CREWE TPO
CREWE – CARDIFF TPO

YEAR	Train.	From	To	VEHICLE. Owning Co.	VEHICLE. Class.	WORKING From	WORKING To	RETURNING BY	
1903	2 45 a.m.	Shrewsb'y	Cardiff 6.12 a.m.	G.W.	Post Office...	Crewe	Cardiff......	7. 5 p.m.	Cardiff ...
				G.W.	Van Third X	,,	,,	11.10 a.m.	,,
				G.W.	Bk.Compo X	Liverpool...	,,	11.10 a.m.	,,
				G.W.	Compo (2) X	,,	,,	7. 5 p.m.	,,
				N.W.	Bk.Compo B	,,	,,	,,	,,
				N.W.	Bk. Van... X	,,	,,	,,	,,
				G.W.	Compo ... X	,,	,,	12.20 a.m.	,,
				G.W.	Parcels Van	M'nchester (Exchange)	,,	,,	,,
				G.W.	Compo ... X	Birk'nhead	,,	11.10 a.m.	,,
				G.W.	Van Third X	,,	,,	12.20 a.m.	,,
				—	Fish Vans S	X Grimsby	,,	—	—
	2 30 p.m. (Mail	Plymouth 7.0 p.m.	Crewe ... Bristol due 11.15 p.m.)	G.W.	Post Office...	Cardiff ...	Crewe	2.45 a.m.	Shr'wsb'ry
				N.W.	Bk. Compo A	,,	Liverpool...	11.50 p.m.	Liverpool
				G.W.	Compo (2) X	,,	,,	,,	,,
				N.W.	Bk. Van X	,,	,,	,,	,,
				G.W.	Third	Plymouth	Exeter	11. 0 a.m.	Bristol
				G.W.	*Third*...WSO	*Plymouth*	*Bristol*	—	—
				G.W.	*Third*......SO	,,	,,	—	—
				N.W.	Bk. Van X	,,	Liverpool...	11.50 p.m.	Liverpool
				G.W.	Bk.Compo(2) X	,,	,,	,,	,,
				W. C.J.S.	Bk. Compo X B	,,	Glasgow ...	4.45 p.m.	Glasgow
				G.W.	Bk.Compo(2) X	,,	M'nchestr	12. 5 a.m.	M'chester
				G.W.	Third X	,,	,,	,,	,,
				N.W.	Bk. Van X	,,	,,	,,	,,
				G.W	Milk Truck S X	,,	Bristol (For Severn Tunnel)		

E On Sunday mornings runs to Plymouth only.

P 7. 0 p.m. Penzance to Truro; 7.45 a.m. thence.
T 7.55 a.m. Penzance to Plymouth.

TABLE 5

CARDIFF – CREWE TPO
CREWE – CARDIFF TPO

YEAR	Train.	VEHICLE. Owning Co.	VEHICLE. Class.		WORKING. From	WORKING. To		BALANCE. Time	BALANCE. From	
1929	**12 10 p.m.** (Mail) Penzance to Crewe (7.20 p.m. ex Bristol) due 11.22 p.m.	G.W.	Post Office 862, 864 or 865	SX	Cardiff.....	Crewe		1.25 a.m. ..	Crewe ..	MX
		G.W.	Mail V No. 838 or 840	†	North Rd...	Bristol		6.18 a.m. ..	Bristol	
		G.W.	Bk. Van	SX	Penzance...	Leeds (Wellington)		8.45 a.m. ..	Bristol	MX
		G.W.	Van Third....	B	Cardiff.....	Liverpool ..		1.25 a.m. ..	Crewe	
		G.W.	Compo		,,	,,		,,	,,	
		G.W.	Van Third....	A	,,	,,		,,	,,	
		G.W.	Bk. Compo ..		Penzance ..	,,		8.17 p.m. ..	,,	
		G.W.	Siphon G		,,	,,		,,	,,	
		LMS	Bk. Van......		,,	Manchester		,,	,,	
		LMS	Compo		,,	,,		,,	,,	
		LMS	Van Third....	A	,,	,,		,,	,,	
		G.W.	Bk. Compo ...	A	,,	Glasgow ...		1.25 a.m. ..	Crewe	
		G.W.	Van	SX	,,	Leeds		3.40 a.m. ..	,,	
		G.W.	Bk. Van	+SX	,,	Sheffield ...	H	10.13 p.m....	York	SX
		G.W.	*Van*	+RR	*Helston* ...	,,	H	,,	,,	RR
		G.W.	Van	+SX	Kingsbridge	,,	H	,,	,,	SX
		G.W.	*Compo*	FO	*Exeter*	*Bristol*		—	—	
		G.W.	Bk. Van	+SX	Trowbridge	Manchester.		3.40 a.m. ..	Crewe	
		G.W.	Siphon C. ...	+	Calne	,,		,,	,,	
	1 25 a.m. Crewe to Cardiff (*Tuesdays to Saturdays*). due 5.12 a.m. *	G.W.	Bk. Compo ...	B	Glasgow ...	Penzance ..	E	12.10 p.m. ..	Penzance ..	
		G.W.	Post Office 862 864 or 865		Crewe	Cardiff.....		7.20 p.m. ..	Cardiff	SX
		LMS	Bk. Van......		Manchester.	,,		12. 5 a.m., ..	,,	
		G.W.	Van Third ...		Liverpool ..	,,		7.20 p.m. ..	,,	
		G.W.	Compo		,,	,,		,,	,,	
		G.W.	Van Third....		,,	,,		,,	,,	
		LMS	Van Third....		,,	Penzance....	E	4.30 p.m. ..	Penzance ..	
		LMS	Compo		,,	,,	E	,,	,,	
		LMS	Bk. Van......		,,	,,	E	,,	,,	
		LMS	Van Third....		Manchester.	,,	E	,,	,,	
		LMS	Compo		,,	,,	E	,,	,,	
		LMS	Bk. Van......		,,	,,	E	,,	,,	
		G.W.	Bk. Van......		,,	Kingswear..		5.40 p.m. ..	Kingswear .	
		G.W.	Van Third....		Birkenhead	Cardiff	C	12. 5 a.m. ..	Cardiff	
		G.W.	Bk. Compo ..		,,	,,	C	2.15 p.m. ..	,,	
		G.W.	Siphon G. ...		Manchester. (Exchange)	,,	D C	4.35 p.m. ..	Plymouth ..	

C 7.40 p.m. Plymouth to North Road, 8.0 p.m North Road to Bristol.
E Off 7-0 a.m. ex Plymouth.
F 9.10 a.m. or 12.0 noon as ordered.
H Detached at Bristol, 7.32 p.m. Bristol to Swindon; 9.5 p.m. thence.
K 12.30 a.m. Crewe to Manchester,.
P 2·15 p.m. ex Cardiff Week-day set.
* G.W. and L.M.S. Car alternate Sundays.

† Also see TABLE 2 regarding 12.10 Penzance – Crewe formation as this train also carries the Plymouth – Bristol TPO coach upon its return working.

TABLE 5

CREWE – CARDIFF TPO
CARDIFF – CREWE TPO

TIMINGS September 1932

	A.M.	P.M.
Shrewsbury	2.05	10.20
Hereford	3.27	9.15
Pontypool Rd.	4.35	8.22
Newport	4.50	7.41
Cardiff	5.14	7.20

COACH ALLOCATIONS

1916 Roster	Nos. 862, 864, 865	
1926 Roster	No. 862 Spares 864, 865	Net 1ns Arms 4ns
1935 Roster	Nos. 801, 802, 803	No apparatus

Following the re-introduction of TPOs after the Second World War all of the vehicles required attention at Swindon Works, the train formation being altered as vehicles became available for traffic. On 1st October 1945 the Great Western TPO was composed of a number of refurbished vehicles as seen in this photograph of stock for the nightly service to Penzance. This formation was to remain until 5th April 1946.
British Railways

PADDINGTON – SOUTH WALES

TABLE 6. South Wales (Night Mail) TPO
TABLE 7. South Wales (North Mail) TPO
TABLE 8. South Wales Bag Tender
TABLE 9. Reading – London Bag Tender

	1903 Table 6 Down p.m.		1903 Table 6 Up a.m.		1903 Table 7 Down a.m.		1903 Table 7 Up p.m.		1916 Table 7 Down a.m.	1916 Table 7 Up p.m.	1932 Table 6 Down a.m.	1932 Table 6 Down a.m.	1932 Table 6 Up a.m.	1932 Table 6 Up a.m.
PADDINGTON	9.15		3.30									9.25	3.25	
READING	↑	Bag Tender	↑	Bag Tender								10.17	2.38	
SWINDON												11.27	1.32	
BRISTOL	↓		↓								12.55			11.57
GLOUCESTER	12.46		12.10		5.35		7.55		5.30	7.54		12.40	12.15	
Grange Court														
Newnham	1.05	2 0	11.54	0 2										
Lydney Junc.	1.18s	a	11.39	0 1h										
NEWPORT											1.47	2.06	11.07	11.16
CARDIFF											2.03	2.43	10.45	10.55
Llantrisant	2.47	1 0			7.10	1 0					STOP			STOP
Bridgend												3.15	10.00	
Port Talbot												3.36	9.40	
Briton Ferry			9.29	1 1g										
Neath												3.50	9.28	
Llansamlet			9.13	1f 1	8.40	1 0	4.16	1 2f						
SWANSEA									9.02	3.55		4.15	9.10	
Gowerton				1 1	9.08	1 0								
Lougher			8.44	0 1d										
Llanelly														
Burry Port	4.34	1 1b	8.27	1 1	9.22	1 0		s0 1						
Kidwelly	4.44	1 1	8.20	1 1	9.07	1 1b		s0 1						
Ferryside	4.48	1 0	8.14	0 1	9.08	1 1b		s0 1						
CARMARTHEN												5.06	8.10	
Clarbeston Rd.	5.56	1 1c	7.05	0 1									p.m.	
NEYLAND	6.40	(a.m.)	6.30	(p.m.)	11.25		1.00							

NOTES

a. Leave 1 empty pouch XT, 3 TO.
b. 1 pouch despatched after 25.04.04.
c. None to be received or despatched after 25.04.04.
d. SSX.
e. None despatched after 13.07.03.
f. None despatched after 5.12.04.
g. None despatched after 25.04.04.
h. 3 pouches SSO.
s. Stops.

TIMETABLE NOTES

TABLE 8. South Wales Bag Tender runs under the timings of Table 6.

TABLE 9. Reading – London Bag Tender runs under the timings of Table 6.

A. 1903 roster shows van No. 748.
B. Not after 6th April 1916.
C. Commencing on 7th April 1916.

APPARATUS WORKING

The 1903 timings include reference to the number of pouches worked at various points along the route. The given number of pouches despatched and received varied according to operational requirements. Table 7 for 1910 (not reproduced) has considerably more pouches being worked and the train making several more stops.

COACH ALLOCATIONS

TABLE 6

Year	Coach Nos.	Nets	Arms
1903	843, 844, 859	1 ns	4 ns
	846, 860, 861	1 ns	4 ns
1920	846, 860, 861	1 ns	4 ns
1926	843, 844	1 os	1 os
	846, 861	–	–
Spares	859	1 os	4 os
	839, 841	1 ns	4 ns
	811	–	–
1935	796, 848, 849	–	–
1949	796, 797, 848	–	–
	849	–	–
1951	796, 848, 849	–	–
1953	796, 797, 848	–	–
	849	–	–

TABLE 7

Year	Coach Nos.	Nets	Arms
1903	274, 275, 276	1 ns	2 ns
1915	864, 865	1 ns	4 ns
1920	839, 841, 843	1 ns	4 ns
	844		

Service ceased 27.10.23.
Coaches transferred to work on Table 10, with timings as per Table 8.

TABLE 8

Year	Coach Nos.	Nets	Arms
1926	846, 860, 861	- ns	4 ns
1935	815, 816, 817	No apparatus	
1951 & 1965	815, 816, 817	No apparatus	

Timings as per Table 8, forming part of the same train as the South Wales TPO.

TABLE 6 — SOUTH WALES (Night Mail) TPO

YEAR	Train.	From Paddington To	VEHICLE.	WORKING. From	WORKING. To	RETURNING BY		Due at Paddington at	
1903 DOWN	9 15 p.m. (Mail) *	Neyland due 6.50 a.m.	Parcels Van	Paddington	P'b'ke Dk. Y	3. 0 p.m	Neyland C	4. 5 a.m.	
			70′ *Parcels Van* S	X ,,	*Neyland* ...Y	*3. 0 p.m.*	,, C	*4. 5 a.m.*	
			50′ OceanBk. Van	X ,,	,, UY	3. 0 p.m.	,, C	4. 5 a.m.	
			Siphon G. ...	,,	Cardiff ZT	,,	,, C	,,	
			P. Post Sorting Van S X	*Paddington*	Neyland ...	*6.30 p.m.*	,,	*3.30 a.m.*	
			Mail Van ...	Gloucester	,,	,,	,,	F	
			70′ *Parcels Van* SO	*Paddington*	,,	,,	,,	*3.30 a.m.*	W
			Van Third X	,,	,,	6.30 p.m.	,,	3.30 a.m.	
			70′ Third (10c) X	,,	,,	,,	,,	,,	
			70′ Third (10c) X	,,	,,	,,	,,	,,	
			70′ First X	,,	,,	,,	,,	,,	
			Van Third (3c)	X ,,	,,	,,	,,	,,	
			Sleeping Car	H ,,	P'broke Dk.	6. 0 p.m.	P'broke Dk.	,,	

C Transferred at Swindon to 5.10 p.m. Penzance.
F Due at Gloucester at 12.10 a.m.
H Runs to Neyland on Saturday nights. If no passengers for Pembroke Dock on other nights, vehicle is worked through to Neyland.
Q Transferred at Swindon to 7.45 p.m. ex Swindon.
T Works through to Taff Vale Line.
U Into Swansea and on by 5.30 a.m. ex Gloucester S.X. S.O. through to Neyland.
W Sunday nights.
Y Detached at Swindon and forwarded thence by 11.37 p.m. Parcels Train.
Z Detached at Swindon and forwarded thence by 11.37 p.m. Parcels Train S.X. On Saturdays only works through to Cardiff on 9.15 p.m. ex Paddington.

YEAR	Train.	From Paddington To	VEHICLE.	WORKING. From	WORKING. To	RETURNING BY		Due at Paddington at	
1903 Sundays	9 15 p.m. (Mail) *	Neyland due 6.50 a.m.	70′ P.P.Sort'g Van	Paddington	Neyland......	6.30 p.m.	Neyland ...	3.30 a.m.	
			Mail Van ...	Gloucester	,,	,,	,,	— R	
			70′ Van	Paddington	,,	3. 0 p.m.	,,	4. 5 a.m.	
			Van Third X	,,	,,	6.30 p.m.	,,	3.30 a.m.	
			Third (10)... X	,,	,,	—	—	—	
			First X	,,	,,	6.30 p.m.	Neyland ...	3. 30 a.m.	MO
			Third (10c) X	,,	,,	,,	,,	,,	
			Third (10c) X	,,	,,	,,	,,	,,	
			Van3rd(3c) X	,,	,,	,,	,,	,,	
			Sleeping Car	,,	P'broke Dk. T	6. 0 p.m.	P'broke Dk.	,,	
			Parcels Van	,,	Swansea......	8.30 a.m.	Fishguard	8. 5 p.m.	
			Compo X	,,	Cardiff	4.45 p.m.	Cardiff ...	,,	K
			Bk. Compo X	,,	Gloucester	9. 0 a.m.	Cheltenham	12.40 p.m.	MO
			Third	,,	Swindon ...	6.30 a.m.	Swindon ...	9.34 a.m.	MO

YEAR	Train.	To Paddington From	Due at Paddington at	VEHICLE.	WORKING. From	WORKING. To	RETURNING BY		
1903 UP	6 30 p.m. (Mail) *	Neyland......	3.30 a.m.	70′ Parcels Van	Neyland......	Paddington	9.15 p.m.	Paddingt'n	SO
				Mail Van ...	,,	Gloucester	12.46 a.m.	Gloucester	
				Van 3rd(3c) X	,,	Paddington	9.15 p.m.	Paddingt'n	
				Third X	,,	,,	,,	,,	
				First X	,,	,,	,,	,,	
				Third X	,,	,,	,,	,,	
				Third X	,,	,,	,,	,,	
				Van Third X	,,	,,	,,	,,	
				57′ OceanBk. Van	,,	,,	,,	,,	
				Sleeping Car	,,	,,	,,	,,	
				Compo	Landore RR	Cardiff or beyond.			
				Bk. Compo ...	,, RR	,,	—	—	
	6 30 p.m. (Mail) *	Neyland......	3.30 a.m.	Siphon G......	Neyland......	**Cardiff ......**	**3.18 a.m.**	**Cardiff ......**	
				Mail Van ...	,,	**Gloucester**	**12.46 a.m.**	**Gloucester**	
				57′ P. Post Sorting Van ...	,,	**Paddington**	**9.15 p.m.**	**Paddingt'n**	
				Van Third(3c)	X ,,	,,	,,	,,	
				70′ First X	,,	,,	,,	,,	
				70′ Third X	,,	,,	,,	,,	
				70′ Third X	,,	,,	,,	,,	
				Van Third X	,,	,,	,,	,,	
				Sleeping Car	Whitland ...	,,	,,	,,	
				Bk. Third RR	*Landore* ...	*Cardiff*	*3.18 a.m.*	*Cardiff*	
1903 UP Sundays	p.m. 6 30 (Mail)	New Milford	3.30 a.m.	Van .... B	New Milford	Paddington	9.15 p.m.	Paddington	
				Mail Van ...	,,	Gloucester	12.46 a.m.	Gloucester	
				Van	,,	Paddington	9.15 p.m.	Paddington	
				Bk. Third (7c)	,,		,,	,,	
				Sleep. C'ch F	,,	,,	,,	,,	
				Tri-Compo ...	,,	,,	,,	,,	
				Van	,,	,,	,,	,,	

TABLE 6 — SOUTH WALES (Night Mail) TPO

YEAR	Train.	From Paddington To	VEHICLE.	WORKING. From	WORKING. To	RETURNING BY		Due at Paddington at	
1905 DOWN	p.m. 9 15 (Mail)	New Milford	*Bk. Third (4c)*	*Padd'ton* G	*W'ym'th L.S.*	*4.10 p.m.*	*W'ym'th L.S.*	*8.20 p.m.*	G
			Tri-Compo ... (Lug B)	,, G	,,	,,	,,	,,	G
			Compo......... (Lug B)	,, G	,,	,,	,,	,,	G
			Bk. Third (4c)	,, G	,,	,,	,,	,,	G
			Van......... J	Paddington	New Milford	6.30 p.m.	New Milford	3.30 a.m.	
			P. Post Sorting Van D	Gloucester	,,	,,	,,	—	E
			Mail Van ...	,,	,,	,,	,,	—	E
			Van	Paddington	,,	,,	,,	3.30 a.m.	
			Tri-Compo ...	,,	,,	,,	,,	,,	
			Bk. Third (7c)	,,	,,	,,	,,	,,	
			Van	,,	,,	,,	,,	,,	
			Sl'ping Car H	,,	PembrokeDk	6. 0 ,,	PembrokeDk	,,	
			6-wh. Parcels Van	,,	Swansea ...	11.40 ,,	Swansea	4.20 p.m	
			Van......... S	,,	*Cardiff*	*11.40* a.m.	*Swansea* ...	*4 20* ,,	
			Tri-Compo...	,,	Oxford ...	7.15 ,,	Oxford ..	9.32 a.m.	
		(Slip)	Tri-Compo..	,,	Henley F		SCW 28		

D Parcel Post Sorting Van not run from Gloucester to New Milford on Sunday mornings.
E Due at Gloucester at 12 10 a.m.
F Slipped at Twyford.
G Tuesdays, Thursdays and Saturdays only.
H Has 4 First Class Sleeping Berths, and 1 Second and 1 Third Class Ordinary Compartments. *Runs to New Milford, instead of to Pembroke Dock, on Saturday nights only.*
J Wingless Van for parcel post.
† Old Oak Common.

YEAR	Train.	From Paddington To	VEHICLE.	WORKING. From	WORKING. To	RETURNING BY		Due at Paddington at	
1905 DOWN Sundays	p.m. 9 15 (Mail) *	New Milford	Van D	Paddington	New Milford	6.30 p.m.	New Milford	3.30 a.m.	
			P. Post Sorting Van	Gloucester	,,	,,	,,	—	E
			Mail Van ...	,,	,,	,,	,,	—	E
			Van	Paddington	,,	,,	,,	,,	
			Tri-Compo ..	,,	,,	,,	,,	,,	
			Bk. Third (7 c)	,,	,,	,,	,,	,,	
			Van	,,	,,	,,	,,	,,	
			Sleeping Car	H ,,	Pemb'ke Dk	6.0 ,,	Pemb'ke Dk.	,,	
			Compo	,,	Swindon	9.15 a.m.	Swindon	11.55 ,,	
			Third	,,	,,	—	—	C	
			Tri-Compo ...	,,	Oxford	7.15 ,,	Oxford F	9.32 ,,	

C Balanced locally.
D Wingless Van for Parcel Post
E Due at Gloucester 12.10 a.m.
F Monday morning.
H Has 4 First Class Sleeping Berths and 1 Second and 1 Third Class Ordinary Compts. *On Saturday nights the car works to New Milford, on other week days to Pembroke Dock.*
J First Class only, to be used on return journey for Ocean Passenger Traffic. Paddington to provide a leader.
L Saturday's train.

YEAR	Train.	To Paddington From	Due at Paddington at	VEHICLE.	WORKING. From	WORKING. To	RETURNING BY	
1905 UP	p.m. 6 30 (Mail).	New Milford	3.30 a.m.	*News Van* ...	*Cardiff* G	*Paddington*	*5.30* a.m.	J Paddington
				Van......... C	New Milford	,,	9.15 p.m.	,,
				P. Post Sorting Van	,, E	Gloucester	12.46 a.m.	Gloucester
				Mail Van ...	,,	,,	,,	,,
				Van	,,	Paddington	9.15 p.m.	Paddington
				Tri-Compo ...	,,	,,	,,	,,
				Bk. Third (7c)	,,	,,	,,	,,
				Sleeping Car	F Pmbke Dk.	,,	,,	,,
				Van....	New Milf'rd	,,	,,	,,
				Third (Corr.)	Penzance H	,,	12. 0 night	L ,,
				Compo .. A	Penzance H	,,	,,	,,
				Sl'p'ng C'r SO	*Plymouth* H	,,	*9.50* p.m.	K ,,
				Bk. Third (3 c)	Penzance H	,,	12. 0 night	,,

A The First Class compartments in this coach are convertible into sleeping berths if required.
C Wingless Van for Parcel Post.
E Parcel Post Sorting Van not run from New Milford to Gloucester on Sundays.
F Has 4 First Class Sleeping Berths, and 1 Second and 1 Third Class Ordinary Compartments.
G Saturdays excepted. Returned from New Milford to London on 10.30 a.m. Sundays.
H 4.45 p.m. Penzance to Bristol; 12.22 a.m. Bristol to Swindon.
J To New Milford by 5.30 a.m. ex Paddington, and New Milford to Cardiff at 4.40 p.m. except Saturdays.
K From London on Friday night.

TABLE 6	SOUTH WALES (Night Mail) TPO

YEAR	Train.	From Paddington To		VEHICLE. No. of Wheels.	Class.	WORKING. From	To	RETURNING BY TRAIN. Time	From		
1905 UP Sundays	p.m. 6 30 (Mail)	New Milford	a.m. 3 30	8	Van.........B	New Milford	Paddington	p.m. 9 15	Paddington		
				8	Mail Van ...	,,	Gloucester	a.m. 12 46	Gloucester		
				8	Van...........	,,	Paddington	p.m. 9 15	Paddington		
				8	Bk. Third (7c)	,,		,,	,,		
				8	Sleep. C'ch F	,,	,,	,,	,,		
				8	Tri-Compo ...	,,	,,	,,	,,		
				8	Van...........	,,	,,	,,	,,		

B Wingless Van for Parcel Post.

F Has 4 First Class Sleeping Berths and 1 Second and Third Class Ordinary Compartment. *On week days the Car works from Pembroke Dock.*

YEAR	Train.	From Paddington To		No. of Wheels	Class.	From	To	Time	From		
1919 DOWN	p.m. 9 15 (Mail)	New Milford		*8*	*Bk. Third (4c)*	*Paddingt'n* **B**	*Weym'th LS*	p.m. *4 10*	*Weym'th LS.*	p.m. *8 20*	B
				8	*Tri-Compo...*	,, **B**	,,	,,	,,	,,	B
				8	*Tri-Compo...*	,, **B**	,,	,,	,,	,,	B
				8	*Bk. Third (4c)*	,, **B**	,,	,,	,,	,,	B
				8	Van......... C	,,	New Milford	6 30	New Milford	a.m. 3 30	
				8	P. Post Sorting Van D	Gloucester	,,	,,	,,	—	E
				8	Mail Van ...	,,	,,	,,	,,	—	E
				8	Van...........	Paddington	,,	,,	,,	,,	
				8	Bk. Third(7c)	,,	,,	,,	,,	,,	
				8	Sl'ping Car H	,,	,,	,,	,,	,,	
				8	Tri-Compo ...	,,	,,	,,	,,	,,	
				8	Van...........	,,	,,	,,	,,	,,	
				4	Poultry Van	,,	Swansea ...	—	—		
				6	*Parcels Van* **S**	,,	*Cardiff*	*1 27*	*Swindon* **G**	p.m. *3 10*	
				8	Tri-Compo...	,,	Oxford ...	a.m. 7 15	Oxford ...	a.m. 9 32	
		(Slip)		8	Tri-Compo..	,,	Henley **F**		**SCW** 28		

C Wingless Van for Parcel Post.

D Parcel Post Sorting Van not run from Gloucester to New Milford on Sunday mornings.

E Due at Gloucester at 12.10 a.m.

F Slipped at Twyford.

H Has 4 First Class Sleeping Berths, and 1 Second and 1 Third Class Ordinary Compartments.

YEAR	Train.	From Paddington To		No. of Wheels	Class.	From	To	Time	From		
1919 DOWN Sundays	p.m. 9 15 Mail)	New Milford		8	Van.........D	Paddington	New Milford	p.m. 6 30	New Milford	a.m. 3 30	
				8	P. Post Sorting Van	Gloucester	,,	,,	,,	—	E
				8	Mail Van ...	,,	,,	,,	,,	—	E
				8	Van...........	Paddington	,,	,,	,,	,,	
				8	Bk. Third(7 c)	,,	,,	,,	,,	,,	
				8	Sleeping Car H	,,	,,	,,	,,	,,	
				8	Tri-Compo ..	,,	,,	,,	,,	,,	
				8	Van...........	,,	,,	,,	,,	,,	
				8	Compo	,,	Swindon	a.m. 9 15	Swindon **F**	11 55	
				8	Third	,,	,,	—	—	C	
				8	Tri-Compo ...	,,	Oxford	7 15	Oxford **F**	9 45	

YEAR	Train.	From Paddington To		No. of Wheels	Class.	From	To	Time	From
1919 UP	p.m. 6 30 (Mail.)	New Milford	a.m. 3 30	8	Van......... A	New Milford	Paddington	p.m. 9 15	Paddington
				8	P. Post Sorting Van	,, C	Gloucester	a.m. 12 46	Gloucester
				8	Mail Van ...	,,	,,	,,	,,
				8	Van...........	,,	Paddington	p.m. 9 15	Paddington
				8	Bk. Third (7c)	,,	,,	,,	,,
				8	Sleeping Car D	,,	,,	,,	,,
				8	Tri-Compo...	,,	,,	,,	,,
				8	Van....	,,	,,	,,	,,
				8	News Van ..	Cardiff **F**	,,	a.m. 5 30	**E** ,,
				8	Bk. Tri-Com.	Penzance **H**	,,	5 30	,,
				8	*Sleeping Car* **SO**	*Plymouth* **H**	,,	p.m. *9 50*	**G** ,,
				8	Bk. Third (3c)	Penzance **H**	,,	,,	,,

A Wingless Van for Parcel Post

B From Gloucester by 5.35 a.m. next day.

C Parcel Post Sorting Van no run from New Milford to Gloucester on Sundays.

D Has 4 First Class Sleeping Berths, and 1 Second and 1 Third Class Ordinary Compartments.

E To New Milford by 5.30 a.m. ex Paddington, and New Milford to Cardiff at 4.40 p.m. except Saturdays.

F Saturdays excepted. Returned from New Milford to London on 10.30 a.m. Sundays.

G From London on Friday night.

H 4.45 p.m. Penzance to Bristol; 12.22 a.m. Bristol to Swindon.

TABLE 6	SOUTH WALES (Night Mail) TPO

YEAR	Train from Paddington.		VEHICLE.		WORKING. From	To		BALANCE.		Due at Paddington at	
1929 DOWN	9 25 p.m. (Mail) to Neyland due 6.45 a.m. (*via Gloucester, Swansea (High St.,) and Carmarthen.*) * V	*60*	*Van ....*	TTh SO	*Paddington .*	*Wey'mth Qy*		*3.45 p.m.*	*Weymouth Qy*	*8.10 p.m.*	TTh SO
		60	*Third........*	TTh SO	,,	,,		,,	,,	,,	TTh SO
		60	*Compo ......*	TTh SO	,,	,,		,,	,,	,,	TTh SO
		60	*Van Third.. A*	TTh SO	,,	,,		,,	,,	,,	TTh SO
			Siphon G....		,,	Swansea....	M	2.25 p.m.	Carmarthen	8.20 p.m.	
			Siphon G	SO	,,	*Llanelly ..*	N	*7.40 p.m.*	*Llanelly ..*	*3.30 a.m.*	*Suns.*
			Mail Van, 843, 844 or 859	SX	Bristol	Carmarthen	F	8.10 p.m.	Carmarthen	to Bristol.	SX
			Post Stowage Van, 846, 860 or 861 ...	SX	Paddington	Neyland ...		6.30 p.m.	Neyland ...	3.30 a.m.	SX
			Siphon G.....	SX	Cardiff.....	,,		7. 0 p.m.	,, to	Cardiff.	MX
		70	*Parcels Van ..*	SO	*Paddington .*	,,		*2.25 p.m.*	,,	*2.25 a.m.*	MO
			Bk. Van......		,,	,,		6.30 p.m.	,,	3.30 a.m.	
		70	Third		,,	,,		,,	,,	,,	
			Sleeping Compo	J	,,	,,		,,	,,	,,	
			Sleeping Car..	SO	,,	,,		,,	,,	,,	*Suns.*
			Compo	L	,,	,,		,,	,,	,,	
			Van Third (3).		,,	,,		,,	,,	,,	
			Siphon G. ...		,,	Cheltenham		10.43 a.m.	Cheltenham	2.30 p.m.	

F Attached at Cardiff off 1.5 a.m. ex Bristol.

J First Class Sleeping Berths trailing.

L First Class compartments leading.

M 8.0 a.m Swansea to Carmarthen.

N 3.15 p.m. Llanelly to Llandovery; 5.0 p.m. Llandovery to Llanelly, Suns.

Q Next trip 5.0 p.m. Paddington to Cheltenham same day.

V This train reverses at Swansea (High St.) and Carmarthen

YEAR	Train from Paddington.		VEHICLE.		WORKING. From	To		BALANCE.		Due at Paddington at	
1929 DOWN Sundays	9 25 p.m. (Mail) to Neyland due 6.45 a.m. (*via Gloucester, Swansea (High St.) and Carmarthen.*) * V		Mail Van, 843, 844 or 859		Bristol	Carmarthen	D	8.10 p.m.	Carmarthen	to Bristol.	E
			Van		Paddington	Cardiff		1.52 p.m.	Cardiff	9.37 p.m.	MO
			Post Stowage Van, 846, 860 or 861 ..		,,	Neyland ...		6.30 p.m.	Neyland ...	3.30 a.m.	
			Siphon G.....		Cardiff	,,		7. 0 p.m.	,,	to Cardiff.	MO
			Brake Van....		Paddington	,,		6.30 p.m.	,,	3.30 a.m.	
		70	Third		,,	,,		,,	,,	,,	
			Sleeping Compo	K	,,	,,		,,	,,	,,	
			Compo	L	,,	,,		,,	,,	,,	
			Van 3rd (3)...		,,	,,		,,	,,	,,	
			Third		,,	Swindon ..		—	—	—	
			Third	+RR	,,	,,		—	—	—	

D Attached at Cardiff off 1.5 a.m. ex Bristol.

E Detached at Cardiff; 10.55 p.m. thence to Bristol.

K First Class Sleeping berths trailing.

L First class compartments leading.

V This Train reverses at Swansea (High St.) and Carmarthen.

YEAR	Train from Paddington.		VEHICLE.		WORKING. From	To		BALANCE.		
1929 UP	6 30 p.m. (Mail) Neyland due 3.30 a.m. (*via Carmarthen, Swansea High Street and Gloucester.*) J *		Mail Van 843, 844 or 859	SX	Carmarthen ..	Bristol	D	1. 5 a.m. ..	Bristol	
			Post Stowage Van 846, 860 or 861	SX	Neyland	Paddington ..		9.25 p.m. ..	Paddington	
			Siphon G.....		,,	,,		8.55 p.m. ..	,,	K
			Brake Van....		,,	,,		9.25 p.m. ..	,,	
		70	Third		,,	,,		,,	,,	
			Compo	P	,,	,,		,,	,,	
			Sleep. Compo	Q	,,	,,		,,	,,	
			Van Third (3).	A	,,	,,		,,	,,	
			Siphon G		,,	,,		8.55 p.m. ..	,,	K
			Van	+SX	,,	B'ham (LMS)	C	1. 5 a.m. ..	Gloucester	
			Siphon G.....		Cheltenham ..	Paddington ..		1. 0 a.m. ..	Paddington	
			Bk. Van......		Gloucester ...	,,		12. 5 p.m. ..	West London	

C Attached at Cardiff off 2.25 p.m. ex Neyland.

D Detached at Cardiff and forward to Bristol at 10.55 p.m.

K 8.15 p.m. Paddington SO

P First Class compartments trailing.

Q First Class Sleeping Berths leading.

YEAR	Train from Paddington.		VEHICLE.		WORKING. From	To		BALANCE.	
1929 UP Sundays	6 30 p.m. (Mail) Neyland due 3 30 a.m. (*Mondays*) (*via Carmarthen, Swansea (High St.) and Gloucester*) M *		Mail Van 843, 844 or 859.		Carmarthen ..	Bristol	H	1. 5 a.m. ..	Bristol ....
			Post Stowage Van 846, 860, or 861.		Neyland	Paddington ..		9.25 p.m. ..	Paddington
			Bk. Van......		,,	,,		,,	,,
		70	Third		,,	,,		,,	,,
			Compo		,,	,,		,,	,,
			Sleeping Car..		,,	,,		,,	,,
			Sleeping Com.	Q	,,	,,		,,	,,
			Van Third (3)	A	,,	,,		,,	,,
			Third		,,	,,		,,	,,
			Bk. Van		Whitland.....	,,	G	—	—
			Siphon G		St. Clears	,,	G	—	—
			Siphon G		Clynderwen ..	,,	G	—	—
			Siphon G		Carmarthen ..	,,	G	—	—
			Siphon G		Llandovery...	,,	G	—	—

G Attached at Cardiff off 3.35 p.m. ex Neyland.

H Detached at Cardiff and forward to Bristol at 10.55 p.m.

M This Train reverses at Carmarthen and Swansea (High St.). Formation shewn in order Train leaves Swansea (High St.)

Q First-class sleeping berths leading.

TABLE 9 — NEW MILFORD – PADDINGTON (North Mail)

YEAR	Train.	To Paddington From	Due at Paddington at		VEHICLE.	WORKING. From	WORKING. To		RETURNING BY		
1903	3 30 p.m. *	Swansea to	Swindon		Wingless Van	Swansea......	Gloucester	T	5.30 a.m.	Gloucester	
					Mail Van ...	,,	,,	T	,,	,,	
					Van Third X	,,	Swindon	L	8.45 a.m.	,,	
					Compo ... X	,,	,,	L	,,	,,	
					Van Third XB	,,	,,	L	,,	,,	
					Van Third X	,,	Paddington	F	3.20 p.m.	Paddington	
					First......... X	,,	,,	F	,,	,,	
				70′	Third X	,,	,,	F	,,	,,	
				70′	Van Third X	,,	,,	F	,,	,,	
1905	p.m. 1 0 (Mail.)	New Milford	11.45 p.m.		Van......... A	New Milford	Gloucester		5.35 a.m.	Gloucester	
					6-wheel Mail Van	,,	,,		,,	,,	
					Bk. Tri-Com. N	,,	,,		11. 0 ,,	Paddington	
					Bk.Third(7c)	,,	,,		5.35 ,,	Gloucester	
					Third MSO	,,	Swindon		—	—	
					Bk.Third(3c)	,,	Paddington		5. 5 p.m.	Paddington	D
					Compo	,,	,,		,,	,,	D
					Bk.Third(4c)	,,	,,		,,	,,	D
1919	p.m. 1 0 (Mail.)	New Milford	p.m. 11 45	8	Van......... A	New Milford	Gloucester		a.m. 5 35	Gloucester	
				6	Mail Van ...	,,	,,		,,	,,	
				8	*Third* MSO	,,	,,		—	—	
				8	Bk.Third(3c)	,,	Paddington		p.m. 5 5	Paddington	B
				8	Compo	,,	,,		,,	,,	B
				8	Third	,,	,,		,,	,,	B
				8	Tri-Compo.	,,	,,		a.m. 10 32	,,	B
				8	Bk.Third(4c)	,,	,,		p.m. 5 5	,,	B

F On from Swindon by 5.0 p.m. Weston-super-Mare.

L 8.30 a.m. Fishguard to Landore; 3.30 p.m. Swansea to Swindon; 2.5 p.m. Swindon to Paddington next day.

T Transferred at Cardiff to 5.30 p.m.

A Wingless Van for parcels post.

D Balanced on 5.35 a.m. ex Gloucester.

N 9.3 p.m. Gloucester to Cheltenham. 1.20 p.m. Cheltenham to New Milford.

TABLE 11
TRURO & FALMOUTH ST.

TIMINGS

1871 Roster

	a.m.	*p.m.*
Truro	dept. 6.50	arr. 5.05
Falmouth	arr. 7.15	dept. 4.35

1903 Roster

Truro	dept. 6.35	arr. 5.50
Falmouth	arr. 7.05	dept. 5.20

COACH ALLOCATIONS

1892 roster. Cornwall Railway van No. 1.
1893 roster. Nos. 500 & 491.

Service ceased August 1916.

TABLE 10
CARMARTHEN & NEWCASTLE EMLYN ST.
North & Night Mails

TIMINGS 1903 Roster

	Night Mail. B. *a.m.*	*a.m.*	*a.m.*		*Day Mail. C.* *p.m.*	*p.m.*
Carmarthen	4.45 ↓	5.20 ↑	5.50	..	1.45	6.15
Carmarthen Jnc.	4.50	5.15	↓	A	↓	↑
Llandyssil			6.50	..	2.45	5.15
Newcastle Emlyn			7.07	..	3.15	4.50

A. Carriage returns empty for the Day Mail.
B. Connects with the South Wales Night Mail.
C. Connects with the South Wales Day Mail.

COACH ALLOCATIONS

1903 Roster. Nos. 490 & 499 with the GWR using one third of the 28 ft vans.

Service ceased 1st May 1904.

4–6–0 *Powderham Castle* approaching Paddington on 15th February 1952, hauling TPO Van No. 816 from the South Wales service. The vehicle, equipped with a late fee posting box, was not fitted with apparatus at this time. *C. C. B. Herbert*

TABLE 12
OXFORD & DIDCOT BAG DUTY

NIGHT MAIL

Oxford	dept. 9.40 p.m.	arr. 11.13 p.m.
Didcot	arr. 10.03 p.m.	dept. 10.50 p.m.

COACH ALLOCATION
One compartment in a 3rd class carriage.

DAY MAIL

Oxford	7.40 a.m. ↑	3.57 p.m. ↓
Didcot	7.15 a.m.	4.22 p.m.

Ceased 21.5.1902.

COACH ALLOCATION
One compartment in a 3rd class carriage.

TABLE 13
READING & LONDON BAG DUTY

See Table 9.

A connection through from the South Wales Night Mail TPO, with the front portion of a Bk van (23 ft) being allocated for mail use with the remainder being used for passengers' luggage.

TABLE 14
SPECIAL AMERICAN & WEST INDIAN MAILS
(Ocean Mails)

For details of the running of these trains reference should be made to the section dealing with Plymouth Millbay where full details of the disposal of the mails are given. Running of these non TPO trains with large quantities of mail and the passenger specials was timed to the arrival and departure of the liners calling at Plymouth.

COACH ALLOCATIONS

1903	862, 863	To be kept at Plymouth Millbay.
1915	821, 822, 823, 824, 837, 862, 863	„
1920	821, 822, 823, 824, 837	„
	839	To be kept at Swindon, used as required.
	844, 863	To be kept at Henley-on-Thames, used as required.
	782, 785, 786, 1128	To be kept at OOC, and used if required.

The service ceased as a TPO between 10th January 1922 and June 1925 but continued as a stowage train until 1962.

TABLE 15
SHREWSBURY – ABERYSTWYTH SC

TIMINGS (Connecting to the T.P.O. only)

	1st January 1865			*Summer 1904*			*Sept. 1932*	
	Down	*Down SSO*	*Up*	*Down SSX*	*Up*	*Down SSO*	*Down*	*Up*
Station	*a.m.*	*p.m.*	*p.m.*	*a.m.*			*a.m.*	*p.m.*
SHREWSBURY	3.30	6.00	9.30	3.20	9.46	3.20	3.25	9.36
WELSHPOOL	4.55	7.05	8.35	4.12	9.00	7.00	4.15	8.50
MONTGOMERY	5.25	7.25	8.17	4.24	8.44	7.13		8.21
Abermule	–	–	8.07	–	–	–		8.14
Newtown	6.10	7.50	8.00	4.41	8.26	7.34	4.39	8.06
Moat Lane Jcn*	6.38	8.03	7.45	4.55	8.11	7.48	4.56	7.55
„ „ „	6.40	8.03	7.50	5.05	8.00	7.50		
Llanidloes	7.00	8.25	7.20	5.27	7.40	8.10		
Brecon				7.45	5.35	10.23		
Carno	7.15	8.35	7.20	5.11	7.52	8.02		7.36
Llanbrynmair	7.30	8.55	7.00	5.20	7.38	8.16		7.20
Cemmes Rd.	8.10	9.10	6.45	5.29	7.26	8.30		7.08
Machynlleth	8.35	9.25	6.30	5.42	7.17	8.45	6.30	6.58
„				5.55	7.20	–		
Barmouth				6.50	5.55			
Pwllheli				c.	4.00			
Glan Dovey	8.50	9.40	6.20	5.50	6.58	8.54		6.50
Ynyslas	9.13	10.00	–	6.02	6.58	9.10		–
Borth	9.23	10.05	6.00	6.02	6.58	9.10		6.25
Llanfihangel	9.30	10.13	–	–	–	–		–
Bow Street	9.40	10.20	5.45	6.11	6.35	9.16		6.20
ABERYSTWYTH	10.00	10.25	5.30	6.20	6.25	9.23	6.20	6.10
					Pass & Mails			a.

NOTES

* Originally known as Caersws Junction.
a. All stations stopping train.
1904 timings appear much as the 1932 times.
c. Some mails to Pwllheli via Dolgelly.

COACH ALLOCATIONS

LNWR coaches were first used on the service until the Cambrian built their own vehicle. The Cambrian coach No. 200 of 1888 replaced the LNWR vehicle No. 4. The second Cambrian vehicle was No. 293 of 1902 which did pass into the GWR stock, but remained on this service as a spare when the GWR allocated No. 863. In 1933 a newer coach was placed in service, No. 797 (L22) and equipped with 1 ns net and 4 ns arms, although apparatus working did not occur. No. 796 was the allocated spare.

No. 293 once displaced from the main service was maintained on the Brecon – Moat Lane service.

Service ceased 23rd September 1939.

APPENDIX No. 1

The following Appendix is drawn from the early 1900s, the figures quoted forming part of the GWR Company's appeal to the Railway & Canal Commission, Royal Courts of Justice, for arbitration on the renewed contract with the Postmaster General for the carriage of mails. It was heard before Mr. Justice Wright between 29th January and 12th March 1903 (8 days) and the judgement was delivered on 7th April.

The GWR had claimed for the period 20th August 1899 to 31st December 1901 £252,571 p.a. (granted £146,606) and from 1st January 1902 £290,618 p.a. (granted 2.1.02 to 22.5.02 £146,606 and from 23.5.03 £135,536 p.a.) but the court did not award the full amount and gave a far from straightforward answer to their claim. This was to reinforce and continue the antagonism between the two parties, although the GWR never refused to renew the contracts.

The evidence for the claim, some of which is reproduced here, provides quite an insight into the cost of running a railway at the turn of the century.

Great Western Railway Company's costs to the Postmaster General in respect of services rendered

As from the 1st January 1902

		Per annum
1.	Conveyance of Mails: calculated at ordinary parcel rates, based upon the traffic at times other than Christmastide	£130,000
2.	Increased carryings of Mails at Christmas as four extra weeks	10,000
3.	Additional service in conveying Ocean Mails: calculated at ordinary parcel rates	6,304
4.	Construction, maintenance, lighting, and haulage of mail vans; and wear and tear of road in their use	18,168
*5.	In respect of control exercised by the Post Office over "Notice" trains at 9*d.* per mile	19,634
†6.	In respect of control exercised by the Post Office over "Agreement" trains at 6*d.* per mile	4,846
7.	Accelerations and additional trains as agreed	8,100
8.	Conveyance of Post Office servants at ordinary fares	24,475
9.	Rent for sites of mail-exchange apparatus and huts	413
10.	Rent and maintenance in respect of gates, paths, &c.	96
11.	Rent for sites of Post Office letter-boxes at stations; and user by public of Company's premises for posting letters in boxes	546
12.	Clearing Post Office letter-boxes at stations	35
13.	Easements for mail-lockers on platforms	10
14.	Conveyance of Mails by omnibus	340
15.	Occupation of Company's platforms, and use of sorting-carriages for office purposes at stations	130
16.	Use of Company's premises for sorting mails	12
17.	Rent of office provided for Post Office servants at Paddington	50
18.	Turning mail vehicles	795
19.	Easement for use of line for walking purposes	40
20.	Contingencies in respect of carrying exceptional mails	500
21.	Exclusive use of passenger-compartments in trains	160
22.	Miscellaneous items	43
23.	Use of Company's premises by Post Office staff	6,524
24.	Running of new Mail-trains between London and Penzance at 5*s.* per mile	59,397
		£290,618

* This figure to be reduced as from May 21st, 1902 (on which date the Post Office relinquished control over certain Notice trains) to £18,704

† This figure to be reduced as from May 21st, 1902 (on which date the Post Office relinquished control over certain Agreement trains) to 3,841

GREAT WESTERN RAILWAY.

Branch Trains under Control.

Train. (1.)	Annual Mileage. (2.)	Annual Earnings, exclusive of Letter Mails. Railway Traffic. As shown by Company's Statement. (3.)	Addition of 34·2 per cent. to bring Traffic taken up to Average for the Year (4.)	Average Railway Traffic. (5.)	Parcel Mails, on the assumption that each Train carries the same Proportion of Parcel Mails as of Letter Mails. (See Statement No. 3.) (6.)	Total. (7.)	Proposed Payment for Conveyance of Mail Bags at ⅔ Newspaper Parcel Rates. (8.)	Proposed Payment for Sorting Carriages (see Table G.P.O. 5). 9.)	Total Earnings, including Mails. (10.)	Average Earnings of Branch Line Trains at 2s. 6d. a Mile. (11.)
Agreement Trains.	Miles.	£	£	£	£	£	£	£	£	£
(1) 9 a.m. Bristol to Plymouth (a)	40,213	?Average Load (b)	—	Average Load.	508	—	258	—	—	5,027
(2) 2.25 a.m. Gloucester to Hereford. (Goods)	10,992	Average Load.	—	Average Load.	58	—	28	—	—	1,374
(3 & 3A) 7.35 p.m. Dolgelly to Chester	22,649	2,005	686	2,691	501	3,192	201	—	3,393	2,831
(4 & 4A) 2.55 a.m. Chester to Dolgelly. (Goods)	22,649	Average Load.	—	Average Load.	404	—	164	—	—	2,831
(5) 5.20 a.m. Llanelly to Llandovery	9,603	560	192	752	121	873	50	—	923	1,200
(6) 6.45 p.m. Llandovery to Llanelly	9,603	820	280	1,100	149	1,249	60	—	1,309	1,200
(7) 6.55 a.m. Llanelly to Llandilo (Sundays)	1,064	78	27	105	Nil.	105	3	—	108	133
(8) 4.45 p.m. Llandilo to Llanelly (Sundays)	1,064	171	58	229	Nil.	229	3	—	232	133
(9) 5.17 a.m. Carmarthen Junction to Newcastle Emlyn	8,084	876	300	1,176	219	1,395	84	128	1,607	1,010
(10) 4.50 p.m. Newcastle Emlyn to Carmarthen Junction	8,084	1,256	430	1,686	200	1,886	79	128	2,093	1,010
(11) 5.30 a.m. Leominster to Kington	5,028	73	25	98	228	326	94	—	420	629
(12 & 12A) 7.40 p.m. Kington to Leominster	5,029	191	65	256	135	391	50	—	441	629
(13) 7.20 a.m. St. Erth to St. Ives	1,561	107	37	144	18	162	7	—	169	195
(14) 6.0 a.m. Par to Newquay (Goods)	6,515	Average Load.	—	Average Load.	60	—	23	—	—	814
(15) 6.42 a.m. Johnston to Milford	1,221	109	37	146	2	148	1	—	149	153
(16) 6.15 a.m. Yeovil to Durston	6,275	176	60	236	91	327	38	—	365	784
(17) 5.50 a.m. Whitland to Cardigan	8,577	429	147	576	72	648	32	—	680	1,072
(18) 5.35 p.m. Cardigan to Whitland	8,577	611	209	820	98	918	42	—	960	1,072
(21) 3.50 a.m. Newton Abbot to Torquay	2,135	240	82	322	30	352	14	—	366	267
(22) 8.56 p.m. Torquay to Newton Abbot (Sundays)	316	95	—(c)	95	Nil.	95	2	—	97	39
(24) 3.0 a.m. Taunton to Chard	5,543	81	—(c)	81	244	325	101	—	426	693
(25) 9.55 p.m. Chard to Taunton	5,543	81	—(c)	81	198	279	80	—	359	693
(26) 10.57 p.m. Cardiff to Bristol	13,888	1,288	—(c)	1,288	372	1,660	157	—	1,817	1,736
(27) 1.0 a.m. Bristol to Cardiff	13,888	4,022	—(c)	4,022	781	4,803	333	—	5,136	1,736
(28) 5.15 a.m. Worcester to Moreton-in-Marsh	8,942	251	—(c)	251	117	368	49	—	417	1,118
Notice Trains.										
E. 6.35 a.m. Truro to Falmouth	4,326	482	165	647	149	796	60	144	1,000	541
F. 5.20 p.m. Falmouth to Truro	4,326	535	183	718	69	787	29	144	960	541
	235,695	14,537	2,983	17,520	4,824	21,314	2,042	544	23,427	29,461

(a) This train has been free from control since the 22nd May 1902.
(b) No figures were furnished by the Company respecting this train.
(c) As the return of the traffic in these cases was taken at a later period of the year than February, no addition has been made.

GREAT WESTERN RAILWAY.—Main Line Trains under Control.

Trains.	Annual Mileage.	Annual Earnings, exclusive of Letter Mails. Railway Traffic. As shown by Company's Statement.	Addition of 34·2 per cent. to bring Traffic taken up to the Average for the Year.	Average Railway Traffic.	Parcel Mails, on the assumption that each Train carries the same Proportion of Parcel Mails as of Letter Mails. (*See* Statement No. 3.)	Total.	Proposed Payment for Conveyance of Mail Bags at ⅔ Newspaper Parcel Rates.	Proposed Payment for Sorting Carriage (*see* Table G.P.O. 5).	Total Earnings, including Mails.	Average Earnings of Main Line Trains at 6*s*. 6*d*. a Mile.
(1.)	(2.)	(3.)	(4.)	(5.)	(6.)	(7.)	(8.)	(9.)	(10)	(11.)
Notice Trains.	Miles.	£	£	£	£	£	£	£	£	£
C. 5.30 a.m. Paddington to Bristol - - -	37,044	9,878	3,378	13,256	2,328	15,584	1,001	348	16,933	12,039
D. 3. 0 p.m. Bristol to Paddington - - -	36,807	11,073	3,787	14,860	1,041	15,901	500	348	16,749	11,962
G. 9.15 p.m. Paddington to New Milford - -	104,149	30,030	10,270	40,300	8,877(*b*)	49,177	3,620	571	53,368	33,848
H. 6.30 p.m. New Milford to Paddington - -	104,149	21,438	7,332	28,770	6,419(*b*)	35,189	2,611	571	38,371	33,848
J. 5.35 a.m. Gloucester to New Milford - -	53,357	12,228	4,182	16,410	886	17,296	412	413	18,121	17,341
K. 1. 0 p.m. New Milford to Gloucester - -	53,255	14,246	4,872	19,118	826	19,944	340	412	20,696	17,308
L. 12.40 a.m. Gloucester to Cheltenham - -	2,298	266	91	357	63	420	25	—	445	747
M. 11.30 p.m. Cheltenham to Gloucester - - -	2,290	265	91	356	56	412	22	—	434	744
N. 10.50 p.m. Didcot to Oxford - - -	3,781	(estimated) 465	159	624	105	729	43	—	772	1,229
O. 9.40 p.m. Oxford to Didcot - - - -	3,781	358	122	480	89	569	37	—	606	1,229
P. 6.15 a.m. Bristol to Plymouth - - -	39,956	13,402	4,583	17,985	1,678	19,663	726	367	20,756	12,986
Q. 2.30 p.m. Plymouth to Bristol - - -	39,956	7,741	2,647	10,388	293	10,681	137	—	10,818	12,986
R. 6.45 a.m. Bristol to Plymouth (Sundays) - -	6,938	665	227	892	114	1,006	46	—	1,052	2,255
S. 12. 0 noon. Plymouth to Bristol (Sundays) - -	6,938	3,252	1,112	4,364	32	4,396	17	—	4,413	2,255
T. 7.20 a.m. Didcot to Oxford - - -	3,242	405	139	544	26	570	10	—	580	1,054
U. 3.50 p.m. Oxford to Didcot - - - -	3,221	319	109	428	11	439	4	—	443	1,047
V. 2.10 p.m. Cheltenham to Swindon - - -	13,743	2,863	979	3,842	159	4,001	77	—	4,078	4,466
Agreement Trains.										
19. 5.55 a.m. Whitland to Pembroke Dock - -	8,530	1,271	435	1,706	117	1,823	41	—	1,864	2,772
20. 6. 0 p.m. Pembroke Dock to Whitland - -	8,530	2,260	773	3,033	80	3,113	30	—	3,143	2,772
23. 3.50 p.m. Plymouth to Bristol and Hereford -	60,535	21,919	7,496	29,415	1,748	31,163	787	703	32,653	19,674
Totals - -	592,500	154,344	52,784	207,128	24,948	232,076	10,486	3,733	246,295	192,562

(*a*) These trains have been free from control since the 22nd May 1902. The aggregate deficiency attributable to them is 2,078*l*.
(*b*) Each of these amounts includes a payment of 472*l*., the payment in respect of the parcel sorting carriage run in the night Mail train in each direction between Gloucester and New Milford.

N.B.—No traffic returns have been given by the Company for the Night Mail Trains which ran under control up to the 31st December 1901. Sir Joseph Wilkinson has stated (Questions 1833–4) that the earnings by the new train of the Company running at 9.50 p.m. from Paddington to Penzance are 7*s*. 4·43*d*. a mile. The Company suggest, although they have given no proof on the subject, that the receipts are 30 per cent. more than by the old mail train. If so, the receipts from the old train were 100/130ths or 10/13ths of 7*s*. 4½*d*., or 5*s*. 8*d*. a mile, exclusive of any receipts for letter mails or parcel mails. The actual letter mails carried by this train, reckoned at two-thirds newspaper parcel rates, produce 6,155*l*. 10*s*. 9*d*., and the payment for Sorting Carriages at the rates proposed by the Postmaster-General would be 1,725*l*. 9*s*. 6*d*., making a total of 7,881*l*., or nearly 1*s*. 4*d*. (1*s*. 3·92*d*.) a mile.

Even without reckoning anything for parcel mails (which are calculated to have brought in at least 11,000*l*. a year), we have thus 5*s*. 8*d*. + 1*s*. 4*d*., or 7*s*. a mile, as compared with the average of 6*s*. 6*d*.

No traffic returns have been given for the old up night Mail, but no doubt it was an equally remunerative train.

GREAT WESTERN RAILWAY.

LOCOMOTIVE DEPARTMENT.

STATEMENT showing the Estimated Cost of Working Post Office Mail Trains between London and Penzance for eight weeks in 1902, based on the general average working expenses for Passenger Train, Half-years December 1900 and June 1901, *plus* 20 %.

MILEAGE—

	Daily
Paddington to Penzance	325½
Penzance to Paddington	325½

651 × 56 = 36,456 Miles.

	No. Required	Prime Cost each	Cost		
		£ s. d.	£ s. d.	£ s. d.	£ s. d.
CAPITAL ACCOUNT.					
Rolling Stock, &c., required.					
Locomotive Department :—					
Tender Engines (including Tenders)	4	2,600 0 0	10,400 0 0		
Add ⅓ for spare and off for repairs	1⅓	2,600 0 0	3,466 13 4		
*Buildings and Turntables at £800 per Engine per annum	5⅓	800 0 0	4,266 13 4		
Total Locomotive Department ...	...	...	...	18,133 6 8	
Carriage Department :—					
8 Wheel Brake Van	2	700 0 0	1,400 0 0		
8 „ Parcels Post Sorting Van	2	490 0 0	980 0 0		
8 „ Mail Tender...	2	711 0 0	1,422 0 0		
8 „ Letter Car	2	852 0 0	1,704 0 0		
8 „ Cape Mail	2	740 0 0	1,480 0 0		
8 „ Stowing Van	2	440 0 0	880 0 0		
8 „ Brake Van	2	700 0 0	1,400 0 0		
8 „ Parcels Post Van	2	490 0 0	980 0 0		
			10,246 0 0		
Add ⅓ for spare and off for repairs	...	...	3,415 6 8		
Total Carriage Department	...	...	...	13,661 6 8	
Total Rolling Stock, &c.	...	...	...	...	£31,794 13 4

* This figure does not include Factories for Construction and Repairs.

	Actual District or General Average or Estimated	General Average Cost per Train Mile: Dec. '00	General Average Cost per Train Mile: June '01	Cost			Cost per Train Mile
		d.	d.	£ s. d.	£ s. d	£ s. d.	d.
WORKING EXPENSES.							
Locomotive Department :—							
Salaries, Office Expenses, &c.	G.A.	·13	·14	21 5 4	21 5 4		·14
Running Expenses.							
Wages of Enginemen and Firemen	„	1·98	1·99	302 5 7	...		1·99
Contributions to Enginemen and Firemen's Society	„	·02	·02	3 0 9	...	...	·02
Wages, Cleaners, Coalmen, &c.	„	·41	·43	63 16 0	...	...	·42
Coal Consumed	„	2·89	3·55	489 2 4	...	...	3·22
Water and Cost of Pumping Maintenance ...	„	·24	·25	37 19 6	...	...	
Oil, Tallow and other Stores	„	·21	·22	33 8 4			·22
Total Running Expenses	...	...	...	...	929 12 6	...	6·12
Repairs and Renewals of Engines and Tenders	„	3·05	3·05	463 5 11	...	...	3·05
Repairs, Engine Sheds and Turntables ...	„	·14	·14	21 5 4	...	...	·14
Gas	...	·10	·11	16 14 2	501 5 5		·11
Total Locomotive Working Expenses	...	...	...			1,452 3 3	9·56
Carriage Department :—							
Repairs and Renewals of Carriages	„	3·15	3·07	472 8 2	...	...	3·11
Total Carriage Expenses	..	...	...	...	...	472 8 2	
Total Locomotive and Carriage Working Expenses	...	...	...	...	..	1,924 11 5	12·67
*Add 20 per cent.	...	...	...	...	...	384 18 3	2·53
						2,309 9 8	15·20
Interest and Depreciation on Capital Account :—							
Estimated cost of Rolling Stock &c., as per opposite Statement, at 4 per cent. on total cost=£1,271 15s. 18d. 8/52 of £1,271 15s. 8d. = ...	...	...	...	...	...	195 13 2	1·28
						£2,505 2 10	16·48

*Of this sum 5 per cent. is for Interest and Depreciation at 7½ per cent. on Land, Buildings and Machinery in Factories at Swindon, &c., also Rates and Taxes on same, and 15 per cent. estimated excess cost of working heavy Mail Trains over general average figures which have been taken in this Statement.

APPENDIX No. 2

1858/1885 Notice and Controlled Trains

As part of the agreement between the Railway Companies and the Postmaster General, the Post Office took powers over various railway operated services which would assist in forwarding the mails to their final destination. 'Notice Trains' were those where the Post Office had complete control over the running of the train, its timings, speed, stopping places and composition, while 'Controlled Trains' were services which the railway had to run at agreed times for the mails but the Post Office did not have overall control over the running of the services. These two categories of train service still exist today.

The schedules are broken into four sections which are as follows:-

1. Mail trains run under the notice of the Postmaster General to the times given and under his direct control. These are virtually the Travelling Post Offices.
2. Lines in the general contract but with additional payment for the services used on those lines. These are the connecting services or services which were not TPOs but carried mails.
3. Lines not in the contract but over which the PMG may use all trains under special arrangements.
4. Lines not in the general contract but over which the PMG may use only certain trains. (As this schedule covers nearly every GWR line it has been omitted.)

SCHEDULE No. 1.

Service	Dispatch and Arrival	London Time	Accommodation to be provided by the Company.
LONDON AND BRISTOL *Night Mail*	To be dispatched from the Railway Station Paddington London for Bristol daily at - - -	8 51 p.m.	A travelling post office carriage or carriages with each of these dispatches fitted up in such a manner as the Postmaster General shall require Also as many letter bag carriages fitted up asaforesaid as may be required by the Postmaster General or any officer of the Post Office
	And arrive at the Railway Station Bristol daily at -	12 35 a.m.	
	To be dispatched from the Railway Station Bristol for London daily at -	12 35 a.m.	
	And arrive at the Railway Station Paddington London daily at - -	4 19 a.m.	
LONDON AND BRISTOL *Day Mail*	To be dispatched from the Railway Station Paddington London for Bristol daily (Sundays excepted) at - - - - -	10 0 a.m.	One compartment of a second-class railway carriage with each of these dispatches, fitted up in such manner as the Postmaster General shall require.
	And arrive at the Railway Station Bristol daily (Sundays excepted) at - -	2 30 p.m.	
	To be dispatched from the Railway Station Bristol for London daily (Sundays excepted) at - -	10 0 a.m.	
	And arrive at the Railway Station Paddington London daily (Sundays excepted) at - - -	2 25 p.m.	
SWINDON AND CHELTENHAM *Day Mail*	To be dispatched from the Railway Station Swindon for Cheltenham daily (Sundays excepted) at -	1 0 p.m.	One compartment of a second-class railway carriage with each of these dispatches fitted up in such a manner as the Postmaster General shall require
	And arrive at the Railway Station Cheltenham daily (Sundays excepted) at -	3 5 p.m.	
	To be dispatched from the Railway Station Cheltenham for Swindon daily (Sundays excepted) at -	9 25 a.m.	
	And arrive at the Railway Station Swindon daily (Sundays excepted) at -	11 18 a.m.	
DIDCOT AND OXFORD *Day Mail*	To be dispatched from the Railway Station Didcot for Oxford daily (Sundays excepted) at -	12 20 p.m.	The Company's guards to take charge of the bags forwarded by these dispatches.
	And arrive at the Railway Station Oxford daily (Sundays excepted) at - -	12 40 p.m.	
	To be dispatched from the Railway Station Oxford for Didcot daily (Sundays excepted) at - -	11 35 a.m.	
	And arrive at the Railway Station Didcot daily (Sundays excepted) at - -	11 58 a.m.	

The SCHEDULE Numbered 1—*continued*

Service	Dispatch and Arrival	London Time	Accommodation to be provided by the Company
GLOUCESTER AND GRANGE COURT *Night Mail*		H. M.	
	To be dispatched from the Railway Station Gloucester for the point of junction of the Gloucester and Dean Forest Railway with the South Wales Railway at Grange Court daily at - - -	2 15 a.m.	One compartment or so much as may be necessary of the inside of a second-class railway carriage with each of these dispatches fitted up in such manner as the Postmaster General shall require
	And arrive at the point of junction of the Gloucester and Dean Forest Railway with the South Wales Railway at Grange Court daily at - - -	2 32 a.m.	
	To be dispatched from the point of junction of the Gloucester and Dean Forest Railway with the South Wales Railway at Grange Court for Gloucester daily at	10 30 p.m.	
	And arrive at the Railway Station Gloucesterdaily at	10 47 p.m.	
GLOUCESTER AND GRANGE COURT *North Mail*	To be dispatched from the Railway Station Gloucester for the point of junction of the Gloucester and Dean Forest Railway with the South Wales Railway at Grange Court daily (Sundays excepted) at - - - - -	6 45 a.m.	The Company's guards to take charge of the bags forwarded by these dispatches
	And arrive at the point of junction of the Gloucester and Dean Forest Railway with the South Wales Railway at Grange Court daily (Sundays excepted) at - - - - -	7 5 a.m.	
	To be dispatched from the point of junction of the Gloucester and Dean Forest Railway with the South Wales Railway at Grange Court for Gloucester daily (Sundays excepted) at - - -	7 [illegible] p.m.	
	And arrive at the Railway Station Gloucester daily (Sundays excepted) at -	7 [illegible] p.m.	

The Company to provide sufficient Engines and the Travelling Post Offices Carriages Letter Bag Carriages Compartments of Carriages in the foregoing Schedule mentioned for the Conveyance of the Mails and Bags of Letters and to convey in such Post Offices and other Carriages the Clerks of the Post Office attending each Despatch and also the Guards appointed and employed by the Postmaster General either when in charge of the Mails and Post Letter Bags or when employed in fetching or returning back from conveying the same and the Inspectors of Mails and other Officers of the Post Office at the hours or times and in manner in the foregoing Schedule mentioned

SCHEDULE No. 2

Service.	Dispatch.	Arrival.	Daily or otherwise.	Accommodation to be provided by the Company
Chester to Oswestry - -	3 35 p.m.	5 0 p.m.	Daily (Sundays excepted).	The Company's guards to take charge of the bags forwarded by these despatches.
Chippenham to Frome - -	2 30 p.m.	3 30 p.m.		
Cirencester to Stroud - -	4 25 p.m.	5 20 p.m.		
Dorchester to Bridport -	5 25 p.m.	6 15 p.m.		
Frome to Trowbridge - -	2 30 p.m.	2 58 p.m.		
Gloucester to Hereford -	2 55 p.m.	4 35 p.m.		
Gloucester to Ross - -	7 55 a.m.	8 40 a.m.		
Henley to Twyford - -	12 55 p.m.	1 10 p.m.		
Reading to Hungerford -	1 10 p.m.	2 15 p.m.		
Trowbridge to Frome - -	12 40 p.m.	1 5 p.m.		
Twyford to Henley - -	11 15 a.m.	11 30 a.m.		
Westbury Junction to Warminster - - -	3 20 p.m.	3 35 p.m.		
Windsor to Paddington - -	11 30 a.m.	12 30 p.m.		
West Drayton to Uxbridge -	10 25 a.m.	10 40 a.m.		
Uxbridge to West Drayton -	11 40 a.m.	11 50 a.m.		
Cirencester to Kemble Junction	10 30 a.m.	10 40 a.m.		
Ditto to ditto - -	1 20 p.m.	1 30 p.m.		
Kemble Junction to Cirencester	10 50 a.m.	11 0 a.m.		
Ditto to ditto - -	1 55 p.m.	2 5 p.m.		

SCHEDULE No. 3

Paddington and Bristol.
West Drayton and Uxbridge.
Slough and Windsor.
Maidenhead and Wycombe.
Twyford and Henley.
Reading and Basingstoke.
Reading and Hungerford.
Didcot and Wolverhampton.
Wolverhampton and Chester.
Gobowen and Oswestry.
Swindon and Cheltenham.
Gloucester and Grange Court.
Kemble and Cirencester.
Chippenham and Weymouth.
Westbury and Salisbury.
Holt and Devizes.
Trowbridge and Bathampton Junction.
Radstock Branch.

LONDON:
Printed by GEORGE EDWARD EYRE and WILLIAM SPOTTISWOODE, Printers to the Queen's most Excellent Majesty.
For Her Majesty's Stationery Office. 1858.

SCHEDULE A.

TRAINS UNDER NOTICE.

	Service.	Down Train. Station.	Time Arrive.	Time Depart.	Up Train. Station.	Time Arrive.	Time Depart.
1	Night Mail to and from Penzance.		P.M.	P.M.		P.M.	P.M.
		Paddington	...	9.0	Penzance	...	5. 0
		Reading	9.50	9.52	St. Erth Junction	5. 9	5.11
		Didcot	10.17	10.22	Redruth	5.32	5.34
		Swindon	10.57	11. 2	Truro	5.53	6. 3
		Chippenham	11.24	11.26	St. Austell	6.28	6.30
		Bath	11.47	11.52	Par	6.38	6.40
	Daily.		A.M.	A.M.	Lostwithiel	6.50	6.52
		Bristol	12.13	12.23	Bodmin Road	7.0	7. 2
		Bridgwater	1.11	1.14	Liskeard	7.23	7.25
		Taunton	1.33	1.38	Saltash	7.51	7.53
		Exeter	2.30	2.40	Devonport	7.59	8. 1
		Teignmouth	3. 3	3. 5	Plymouth	8.10	8.23
		Newton Abbot	3.15	3.22	Totnes	9. 9	9.11
		Plymouth	4.27	4.40	Newton Abbot	9.29	9.36
		Saltash	4.50	4.51	Teignmouth	9.45	9.47
		Liskeard	5.18	5.20	Dawlish	9.54	9.56
		Bodmin Road	5.36	5.38	St. Thomas	10.14	10.17
		St. Austell	6. 0	6. 2	Exeter (St. David's)	10.20	10.30
		Truro	6.29	6.35	Taunton	11.20	11.25
		Redruth	6.53	6.55	Bridgwater	11.44	11.47
		Camborne	7. 3	7. 5		A.M.	A.M.
		St. Erth Junction	7.21	7.23	Bristol	12.35	12.45
		Penzance	7.35	...	Bath	1. 3	1. 5
					Chippenham	1.28	1.30
					Swindon	1.55	2. 0
					Steventon	2.28	2.30
					Didcot	2.37	2.40
					Reading	3. 4	3. 9
					Paddington	4.0	...
2	Day Mail to and from Bristol.		A.M.	A.M.		P.M.	P.M.
		Paddington	...	5.30	Bristol	...	3.0
		*Reading	6.25	6.30	Bath	3.17	3.20
		Didcot	6.56	7. 1	Swindon	4. 5	4.10
		Swindon	7.39	7.49	Didcot	4.44	4.47
	Week Days.	Chippenham	8.12	8.16	Westbourne Park	5.50	5.55
		Bath	8.36	8.40	Paddington	6.0	...
		Bristol	9.0	...			
3	Falmouth Night Mail. Daily.		A.M.	A.M.		P.M.	P.M.
		Truro	...	6.40	Falmouth	...	5.25
		Penryn	6.52	6.54	Penryn	5.33	5.34
		Falmouth	7. 2	...	Truro	5.51	...

*NOTE.—The train now stops at Slough at 5.57, but may not be required to do so in the summer.

	Service.	Down Train. Station.	Time Arrive.	Time Depart.	Up Train. Station.	Time Arrive.	Time Depart.
4	Night Mail to and from South Wales.		P.M.	P.M.		P.M.	P.M.
		Paddington	...	9.15	New Milford	...	5.0
		Reading	10. 5	10.10	Johnston	5.13	5.14
		Didcot	10.37	10.40	Haverfordwest	5.22	5.24
		Swindon	11.15	11.20	Clynderwen	5.45	5.46
		Kemble	11.44	11.45	Whitland	5.55	6. 0
			A.M.	A.M.	Carmarthen Junction	6.25	6.30
		Stroud	12. 8	12.11	Llanelly	7. 2	7. 4
	Daily	Gloucester	12.35	12.50	Landore Junction	7.28	7.35
		Lydney	1.23	1.25	Neath	7.50	7.54
		Chepstow	1.38	1.40	Port Talbot	8. 3	8. 4
		Newport	2. 8	2.13	Bridgend	8.27	8.30
		Cardiff	2.33	2.40	Cardiff	9.0	9. 5
		Bridgend	3.12	3.15	Newport	9.23	9.26
		Port Talbot	3.39	3.40	Chepstow	9.51	9.54
		Neath	3.53	3.58	Gloucester	10.35	10.50
		Landore Junction	[illegible]	4.19	Stroud	11.12	11.15
		Llanelly	4.42	4.44	Kemble	11.44	11.45
		Carmarthen Junction	5.16	5.21		A.M.	A.M.
		Whitland	5.48	5.51	Swindon	12.10	12.15
		*Haverfordwest	6.21	6.24	Didcot	12.50	12.55
		Johnston	6.37	6.40	Reading	1.22	1.27
		New Milford	6.58	...	Paddington	2.25	...
5	North Mail to and from S. Wales		A.M.	A.M.		P.M.	P.M.
		Gloucester	...	5.15	New Milford	...	1. 5
		Newnham	5.32	5.33	Johnston	1.17	1.18
		Lydney	5.47	5.49	Haverfordwest	1.27	1.29
		Chepstow	6. 2	6. 3	Clarbeston Road	1.40	1.41
		Newport	6.27	6.31	Clynderwen	1.52	1.53
	Week Days	Cardiff	6.49	6.54	Whitland	2. 3	2. 9
		Bridgend	7.24	7.27	St. Clears	2.19	2.23
		Port Talbot	7.47	7.48	Carmarthen Junction	2.38	2.45
		Briton Ferry	7.55	7.56	Ferryside	2.56	2.57
		Neath	8. 1	8. 5	Kidwelly	3. 6	3. 7
		Landore Junction	8.20	8.30	Pembrey	3.17	3.18
		Cockett	8.40	8.41	Llanelly	3.27	3.29
		Gower Road	8.50	8.51	Loughor	3.37	3.38
		Loughor	8.57	8.58	Gower Road	3.43	3.44
		Llanelly	9. 8	9.10	Cockett	3.53	3.54
		Pembrey	9.19	9.20	Landore Junction	4. 2	4. 9
		Kidwelly	9.29	9.30	Neath	4.22	4.27
		Ferryside	9.39	9.43	Briton Ferry	4.33	4.34
		Carmarthen Junction	9.55	10. 5	Port Talbot	4.42	4.44
		St. Clears	10.20	10.21	Pyle	4.56	4.57
		Whitland	10.32	10.37	Bridgend	5.10	5.14
		Clynderwen	10.48	10.49	Pencoed	5.22	5.23
		Clarbeston Road	11. 2	11. 3	Llantrissant	5.34	5.36
		Haverfordwest	11.13	11.15	Peterston	5.43	5.44
		Johnston	11.27	11.28	St. Fagans	5.50	5.51
		New Milford	11.40	...	Ely	5.56	5.57
					Cardiff	6. 2	6.10
					Newport	6.30	6.35
					Chepstow	7.0	7. 2
					Lydney	7.16	7.18
					Newnham	7.32	7.37
					Gloucester	7.55	...

* NOTE.—This train now stops at Clynderwen on Sunday mornings.

SCHEDULE A.—(*Continued.*)

	Service.	Down Train. Station.	Time Arrive.	Time Depart.	Up Train. Station.	Time Arrive.	Time Depart.
6	Gloucester & Cheltenham Night Mail		A.M.	A.M.		P.M.	P.M.
		Gloucester	...	12.55	Cheltenham	...	10.25
		Cheltenham	1.10	...	Gloucester	10.40	...
	Daily (Mondays excepted).				Daily (Sundays excepted)		
	Oxford and Didcot Night Mail Week days		P.M.	P.M.		P.M.	P.M.
		Didcot	...	10.45	Oxford	...	9.15
		Culham	10.51	10.52	Radley	9.24	9.26
		Radley	10.58	11.0	Culham	9.32	9.33
		Oxford	11.10	...	Didcot	9.40	...
7	Oxford and Didcot Night Mail Sundays		P.M.	P.M.		P.M.	P.M.
		Didcot	...	10.45	Oxford	...	9.45
		Culham	10.51	10.52	Radley	9.54	9.55
		Radley	10.58	11.0	Culham	10. 2	10. 3
		Oxford	11.10	...	Didcot	10.10	...
8	Bristol and Plymouth North Mail		A.M.	A.M.		P.M.	P.M.
		Bristol	...	6.15	Plymouth	...	2.30
		Highbridge	6.55	6.57	Plympton	2.43	2.44
		Bridgewater	7. 8	7.11	Ivybridge	3. 1	3. 3
		Durston	7.22	7.26	Kingsbridge Road	3.10	3.12
		Taunton	7.37	7.42	Totnes	3.28	3.30
		Tiverton Junction	8. 7	8.11	Newton Abbot	3.50	3.56
		Exeter	8.32	8.40	Teignmouth	4. 6	4. 8
	Week days	Starcross	8.59	9. 1	Dawlish	4.15	4.17
		Dawlish	9. 9	9.11	Starcross	4.25	4.27
		Teignmouth	9.19	9.21	Exeter	4.47	4.55
		Newton Abbot	9.31	9.39	Taunton	5.39	5.43
		Totnes	9.56	9.58	Bridgwater	5.59	6. 3
		Ivybridge	10.24	10.26	Bristol	6.45	...
		Plymouth	10.48	...			

SCHEDULE A.—(*Continued.*)

	Service.	Down Train. Station.	Time Arrive.	Time Depart.	Up Train. Station.	Time Arrive.	Time Depart.
8	Bristol and Plymouth North Mail		A.M.	A.M.		P.M.	P.M.
		Bristol	...	6.30	Plymouth	...	12.40
		Nailsea	6.45	6.46	North Road	12.43	12.44
		Yatton	6.54	6.55	Mutley	12.45	12.46
		Puxton	7. 3	7. 4	Plympton	12.53	12.55
		Worle	7. 9	7.10	Cornwood	1. 9	1.10
	Sundays	Weston-super-Mare	7.16	7.19	Ivybridge	1.15	1.17
		Highbridge	7.34	7.35	Kingsbridge Road	1.23	1.25
		Bridgwater	7.47	7.49	Brent	1.31	1.32
		Durston	8.0	8.3	Totnes	1.47	1.49
		Taunton	8.14	8.18	Newton Abbot	2. 9	2.17
		Wellington	8.32	8.34	Teignmouth	2.27	2.29
		Tiverton Junction	8.51	8.54	Dawlish	2.37	2.39
		Collumpton	9.0	9. 1	Starcross	2.47	2.49
		Hele and Bradninch	9.10	9.11	Exminster	2.57	2.58
		Stoke Canon	9.22	9.24	St. Thomas	3. 7	3.10
		Exeter	9.32	9.47	Exeter	3.14	3.30
		St. Thomas	9.50	9.52	Hele and Bradninch	3.45	3.46
		Exminster	9.59	10.0	Collumpton	3.55	3.56
		Starcross	10. 8	10.10	Tiverton Junction	4. 3	4. 5
		Dawlish	10.18	10.20	Wellington	4.21	4.23
		Teignmouth	10.28	10.30	Norton Fitzwarren	4.33	4.35
		Newton Abbot	10.40	10.46	Taunton	4.40	4.44
		Totnes	11. 5	11. 7	Durston	4.55	4.56
		Brent	11.26	11.27	Bridgwater	5. 6	5. 8
		Kingsbridge Road	11.33	11.35	Highbridge	5.20	5.22
		Ivybridge	11.42	11.44	Weston-super-Mare	5.37	5.40
		Cornwood	11.50	11.51	Yatton	5.54	5.56
			P.M.	P.M.	Nailsea	6. 5	6. 6
		Plympton	12. 3	12. 5	Bedminster	6.19	6.22
		Mutley	12.12	12.13	Bristol	6.25	...
		North Road	12.14	12.15			
		Plymouth	12.24	...			
9	Chelt'nham to Swindon Day Mail.		P.M.	P.M.			
		Cheltenham	...	1.55			
		Churchdown	2. 3	2. 6			
		Gloucester	2.13	2.30			
	Week Days	Stroud	2.50	2.53			
		Kemble	3.18	3.22			
		Swindon	3.45	...			
10	Oxford and Didcot Day Mail. Week Days		A.M.	A.M.		P.M.	P.M.
		Didcot	...	7.15	Oxford	...	3.57*
		Culham	7.21	7.22			
		Radley	7.28	7.30			
		Oxford	7.40	...	Didcot	4.22	...

*NOTE.—The Post Office at present use the train leaving Oxford at 4.5 p.m., and will continue to use it as long as it runs at or about that time in lieu of the train shewn at 3.57, but this latter train is retained in accordance with the original Notice as shewing that the Company are under obligation to run a train from Oxford to Didcot at or about that time in connection with the 3.0 p.m. mail train from Bristol to London shewn above.

SCHEDULE B.

	From.	To.	Depart.	Arrive.	Remarks.
1	Bristol	Plymouth	9.15 a.m.	2.20 p.m.	Week Days
2 Goods Train.	Gloucester	Hereford	2.25 a.m.	4.30 a.m.	Week Days
	Do.	Do.	2.25 a.m.	4.35 a.m.	Sundays
3	Dolgelly	Chester	7.35 p.m.	10.23 p.m.	Week Days
	Chester	Dolgelly	2.45 a.m.	7.30 a.m.	
	Dolgelly	Chester	6.55 p.m.	9.55 p.m.	Sundays
	Chester	Dolgelly	2.45 a.m.	8.0 a.m.	
4	Llanelly	Llandovery	5.25 a.m.	7.46 a.m.	Week Days
	Llandovery	Llanelly	5.20 p.m.	6.52 p.m.	
	Llanelly	Llandilo	6.55 a.m.	7.51 a.m.	Sundays
	Llandilo	Llanelly	4.45 p.m.	5.45 p.m.	
5	Carmarthen Junction	Cardigan	5.30 a.m.	10.0 a.m.	On Week Days between Llandyssil and Cardigan the service is performed by coach. On Sundays the service is performed throughout by coach.
	Cardigan	Carmarthen Junction	1.25 p.m.	6.19 p.m.	
6	Leominster	Kington	5.30 a.m.	6.35 a.m.	Daily
	Kington	Leominster	7.40 p.m.	8.15 p.m.	Week Days
	Kington	Leominster	7.45 p.m.	8.20 p.m.	Sundays
7	St. Erth	St. Ives	7.30 a.m.	7.45 a.m.	Daily
8 Goods Train.	Par	Newquay	6.13 a.m.	8.15 a.m.	Week Days To wait half an hour for mail train if necessary.
9	Johnston*	Milford	7.0 a.m.	7.15 a.m.	Week Days
10	Yeovil	Durston	6.30 a.m.	7.14 a.m.	Week Days

* NOTE.—If this Train be taken off by the Company at any time during the continuance of the Contract, they shall make an allowance to the Postmaster General for the period during which the Train does not run, at the rate of £20 per annum.

13

SCHEDULE C.

FROM	TO
Paddington	Penzance (including the Weston-super-Mare Loop)
Southall	Brentford
West Drayton	Uxbridge
Slough	Windsor
Maidenhead	Oxford (Kennington Junc. via Thame)
Princes Risborough	Aylesbury
Twyford	Henley
Reading	Basingstoke
Ditto	Bathampton (via Holt Junction)
Moulsford	Wallingford
Didcot	Newbury
Savernake	Marlborough
Uffington	Faringdon
Swindon	Highworth
Dauntsey	Malmesbury
Chippenham	Calne
Thingley Junction	Weymouth
Westbury	Salisbury
Maiden Newton	Bridport
Bristol	New Passage
Ditto	Portishead
Ditto	Frome (via Radstock)
Hallatrow	Camerton
Yatton	Witham
Ditto	Clevedon
Durston	Yeovil—Pen Mill
Taunton	Chard
Ditto	Minehead
Ditto	Barnstaple
Tiverton Junction	Hemyock
Ditto	Tiverton
Newton Abbot	Moretonhampstead
Newton Abbot	Kingswear
Heathfield	Ashton
Churston	Brixham
Totnes	Ashburton
Mutley	Launceston
Horrabridge	Princetown
Fowey	Newquay
Par	St. Blazey
St. Dennis Junction	Burngullow
Ditto	Melangoose Mill
Tolcarn Junction	Treamble
Bugle	Carbis
Truro	Falmouth
St. Erth	St. Ives
Didcot	Wellington (Salop)
Shrewsbury	Chester
Radley	Abingdon
Oxford	Shrewsbury (via Worcester)
Yarnton	Fairford

14

SCHEDULE C.—(*Continued.*)

FROM	TO
Chipping Norton Junction	Chipping Norton
Ditto	Cheltenham
Honeybourne	Hatton
Bearley	Alcester
Wolverhampton	Bushbury Junction
Kidderminster	Bewdley
Droitwich Junction	Stoke Works Junction
Hartlebury Junction	Bilston
Netherton	Halesowen
Stourbridge Junction	Handsworth Junction
Ditto	Stourbridge
Dudley	West Bromwich
Craven Arms (Marsh Farm Junction)	Wellington (via Buildwas and Ketley Junction)
Madeley Junction	Lightmoor
Wellington (Salop)	Nantwich Junction
Gobowen	Oswestry
Ruabon	Blaenau Festiniog
Bala	Dolgelly
Wrexham	Minera
Moss Valley Line near Wrexham	
Tenbury	Bewdley
Leominster	New Radnor
Titley	Presteign
Ditto	Eardisley
Hereford	Worcester
Bransford Road	Bromyard
Swindon	New Milford
Kemble Junction	Cirencester
Gloucester	Cheltenham
Hereford	Grange Court
Ditto	Newport
Ross	Swansea
Monmouth	Coleford
Wyesham Junction	Wye Valley Junction, Chepstow
Portskewett Junction	Portskewett
Bilson	Bullo Pill
Monmouthshire Railways	Eastern and Western Valleys Lines and Branches
Llynvi & Ogmore Railways	Bridgend to Nantymoel
	Tondû to Abergwynfi
	Brynmenin, Pencoed, Blackmill, and Porthcawl Branches
Llanelly Railway	Llanelly to Llandilo and Brynamman and Mountain Branches
Landore (Low Level)	Morriston
Ditto (High Level)	Swansea (High Street)
Carmarthen Junction	Llandyssil
Johnston	Milford
Hirwain	Merthyr
Ely Valley Railway	Llantrissant to Dinas, Clydach Vale, Hendreforgan, and Gilfach
Awre Junction	Howbeach

15

These schedules were to remain in force until the 1st World War with the exception of the following services which from 21st May 1902 the PMG no longer wished to control.

12.55 a.m.	Gloucester to Cheltenham	(Schedule A No. 6)
10.25 p.m.	Cheltenham to Gloucester	(Schedule A No. 6)
1.55 p.m.	Cheltenham to Swindon	(Schedule A No. 9)
7.15 a.m.	Didcot to Oxford	(Schedule A No. 10)
3.57 p.m.	Oxford to Didcot	(Schedule A No. 10)
9.15 a.m.	Bristol to Plymouth	(Schedule B No. 1)

LINESIDE APPARATUS CLEARANCES

1. GROUND NET ONLY

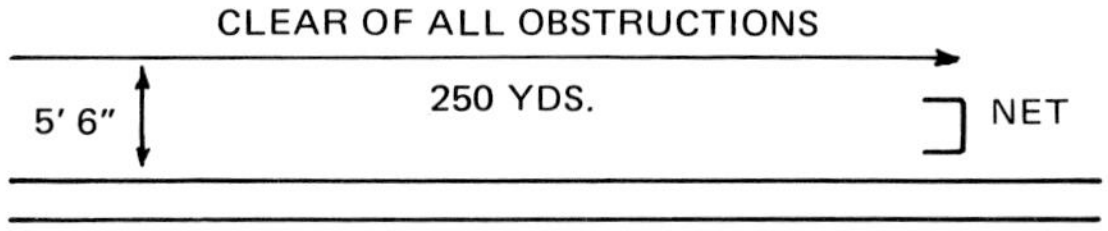

No limit of clearance need be laid down following net apparatus point.

2. WAYSIDE STANDARD ONLY

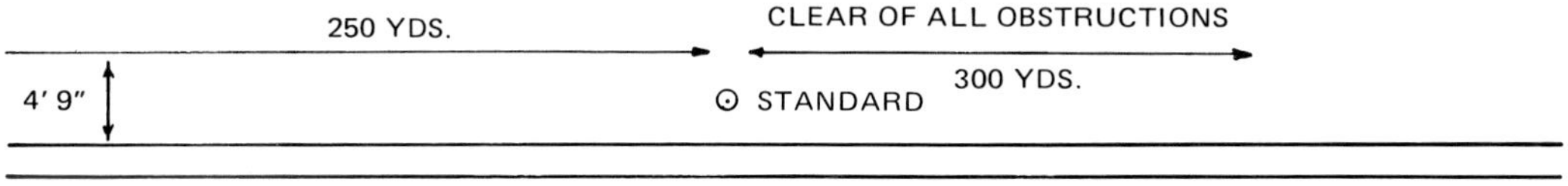

3. WAYSIDE NET AND STANDARD

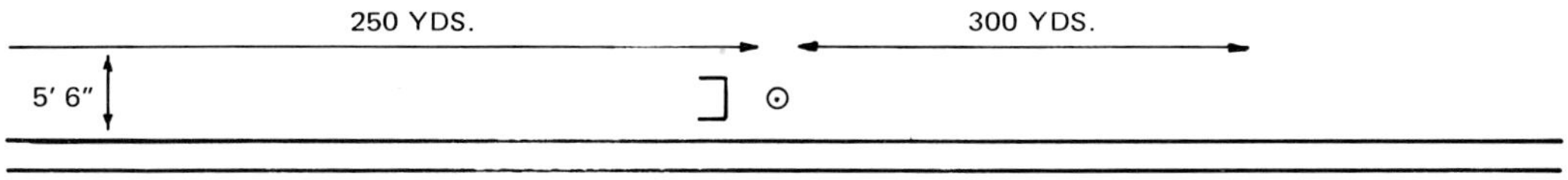

4. TWO WAYSIDE STANDARDS AND A NET

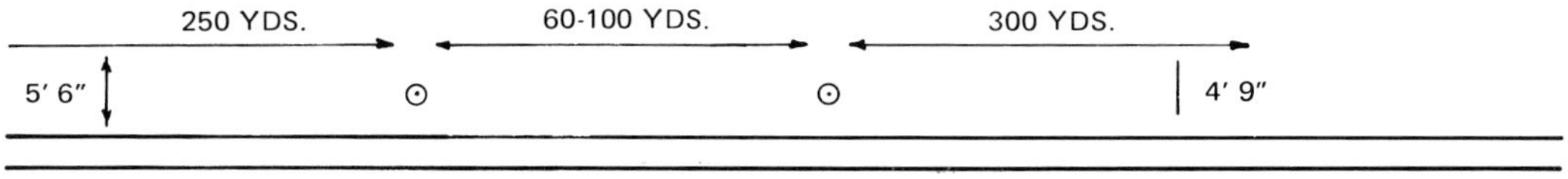

5. THREE WAYSIDE STANDARDS AND A NET

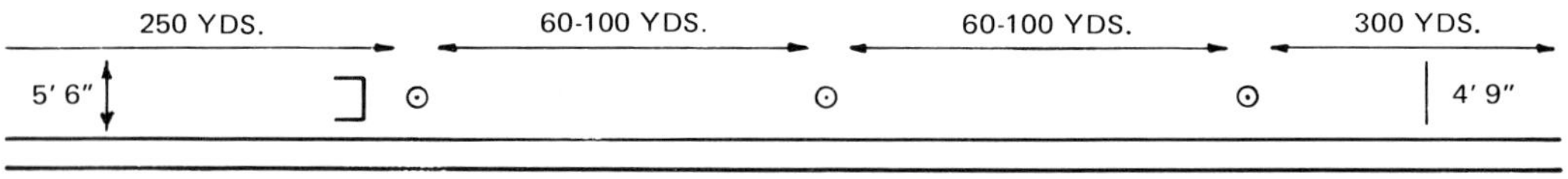

6. WAYSIDE APPARATUS POINT BETWEEN RUNNING LINES

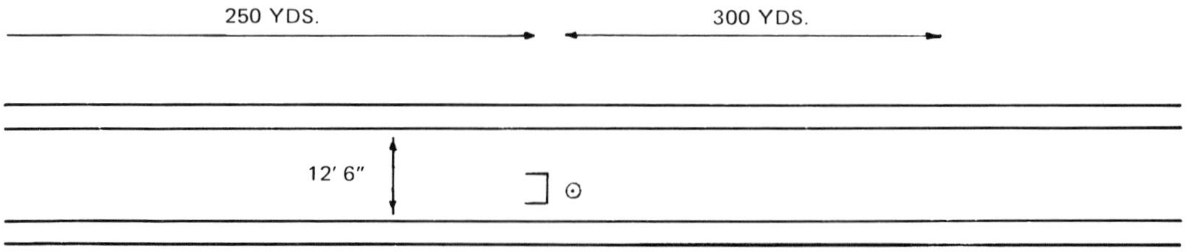

HUT NET AND STANDARD CLEARANCES TO BE MAINTAINED FOR EACH ADDITIONAL SET OF STANDARDS

DIRECTION OF TRAVEL →

APPENDIX No. 3 GWR APPARATUS LOCATIONS

No.	Location	Date
1.	Abergavenny	
2.	Bath	
3.	Brent	
4.	Bridgwater	
5.	Bristol	
6.	Briton Ferry	1863
7.	Bodmin Road	
8.	Burry Port	
9.	Camborne	
10.	Challow	(1876)
11.	Chippenham	(1876)
12.	Cholsey Bridge	1864
13.	Clarbeston Road	
14.	Cullompton	(1876)
15.	Corsham	(1876)
16.	Exeter	
17.	Ferryside	
18.	Dawlish	1876
19.	Didcot	1876
20.	Faringdon Road	1859
21.	Flax Bourton	
22.	Grampound Road	(1876)
23.	Gowerton	
24.	Hayes	1930
25.	Hayle	
26.	Hewish	1876
27.	Highbridge	1876
28.	Highworth Junc.	
29.	Ivybridge	(1876)
30.	Kidwelly	1864
31.	Langford Bridge	
32.	Leominster	
33.	Liskeard	
34.	Llantrisant	(1876)
35.	Llansamlet	
36.	Lostwithiel	(1876)
37.	Ludlow	
38.	Lydney Junc.	
39.	Loughor	
40.	Maidenhead	1859
41	Marazion	1914
42.	Nailsea	
43.	Newton Abbot	
44.	Newnham	
45.	Par	(1876)
46.	Perranwell	1871
47.	Penzance	
48.	Plympton	(1876)
49.	Reading	(1876)
50.	Redruth	
51.	Saltash	
52.	Scorrier	1914
53.	Shrivenham	1864
54.	Slough	1859
55.	Southall	(1876)
56.	Steventon	
57.	St. Austell	
58.	St. Clears	1863
59.	St. German's	(1876)
60.	Swindon	
61.	Taunton	
62.	Teignmouth	
63.	Tiverton Junc.	1869
64.	Totnes	(1876)
65.	Truro	
66.	Twyford	1864
67.	Wallingford Road	1859
68.	Wantage Road	
69.	Wellington	(1876)
70.	West Drayton	1859
71.	Weston Junc.	1869
72.	Wootton Bassett	(1876)
73.	Yatton	1864

Dates shown are for first installation. Dates in brackets are unconfirmed.

LOCATION DESCRIPTIONS

	LOCATION	DOWN JOURNEY	UP JOURNEY
1.	ABERGAVENNY	Going North – 250 yds, north of the station. After passing Pontypool Road observe 3 stations, pass under 2 bridges, run by sidings and through Abergavenny Junction Station. At the end of the platform lower net. 1 standard.	(No apparatus going south)
2.	BATH		
3.	BRENT	990 yds, east of the station. After Totnes observe tunnel, fix on, pass under bridge, lower net, extend arms after white board. 1 standard, 1 net.	Observe Wrangaton station, run through Brent station, pass under one bridge and at the decline of the cutting lower net. 1 standard.
4.	BRIDGWATER	286 yds. west of the station. Observe Dunball station, after one bridge fix on, pass through Bridgwater station and under one bridge, then lower net and extend arms. 1 standard, 1 net.	342 yds. west of the station. After Dunston station run under 3 bridges, fix on, pass over river bridge. At commencement of carriage shed lower and extend. 1 standard, 1 net.
5.	BRISTOL		
6.	BRITON FERRY	(No apparatus on the down journey.)	550 yds. east of the station. Observe Briton Ferry siding, run through station and by two signal posts, pass parapets of bridge, then lower. (1910) 1 standard.
7.	BODMIN ROAD		
8.	BURRY PORT	411 yds. west of the station. After Llanelly notice long sea wall, at side line fix on, pass through station and under bridge, then extend. (1 standard) 1 net. (1910)	400 yds. west of the station. Pass under 3 bridges and at small bridge over railway line lower net. 1 standard (1 net) (1910)

	LOCATION	DOWN JOURNEY	UP JOURNEY
9.	CAMBORNE	850 yds. west of the station. After passing Carn Brea station fix on, run through Camborne station, notice iron railings, pass under one bridge and then lower and extend. 1 standard, 1 net.	After Gwinear Road notice viaduct, fix on, pass two parapets of bridges then lower and extend. 1 standard, 1 net.
10.	CHALLOW		
11.	CHIPPENHAM	600 yds. west of station. Three miles west of Dauntsey observe viaduct. Notice side lines, signal cabin with level crossing, fix on, pass through Chippenham station and over long stone viaduct, at white signal board lower and extend.	(No apparatus on the up journey.)
12.	CHOLSEY BRIDGE	780 yds. east of the station. After Reading observe 2 stations, pass over water trough and through Goring Station, fix on, run over River Thames, pass under next bridge then extend. 1 net. (1924)	865 yds. east of the station. After Didcot station observe side line, fix on, run through Cholsey & Moulsford station and by goods shed, pass signal post erected next to main line, lower and extend. 1 standard, 1 net.
13.	CLARBESTON RD.	478 yds. east of the station. After leaving Clynderwen station pass over 2 rivers and under one bridge, at next bridge, with cottage close to line, fix on, at WSB extend. 1 net.	(No apparatus on the up journey.)
14.	CULLOMPTON	490 yds. west of the station. After working Tiverton Junction fix on, pass through Cullompton station under one bridge and over iron bridge, at white signal board lower and extend. 1 standard, 1 net.	488 yds. west of the station. Observe Stoke Cannon, Silveston and Hele & Bradninch stations, run under two bridges, fix on, pass under next bridge and at white signal board lower and extend. 2 standards, 1 net.
15.	CORSHAM	(No apparatus on the down journey.)	910 yds. east of the station. After passing through Box tunnel fix on, pass through Corsham station and under one bridge then lower and extend. 1 standard, 1 net.
16.	EXETER		
17.	FERRYSIDE	218 yds. west of the station Fix on at sea wall, pass through station and by end of platform then extend. 1 net.	375 yds. east of the station. Pass over water trough, observe side lines, run through station and by level crossing gates then lower net. 1 standard.
18.	DAWLISH	265 yds. east of the station. After passing Starcross station observe Warren Halt station, fix on, pass under footbridge and at white signal board against sea wall extend. 1 net.	240 yds. east of the station. Run through Dawlish station, at end of platform lower net. 1 standard.
19.	DIDCOT		
20.	FARINGDON ROAD		
21.	FLAX BOURTON	650 yds. west of the station. Observe short tunnel, fix on, pass through station and under 1 bridge, extend 1 arm. 1 net.	(No apparatus on the up journey.)

	LOCATION	DOWN JOURNEY	UP JOURNEY
22.	GRAMPOUND ROAD	600 yds. east of station. After passing Burngullow station run over two stone viaducts, fix on, pass under next bridge, and at white signal board lower and extend. RELOAD QUICKLY: after passing over small bridge with iron railings 30 yds. west of first net extend for second net. 1 standard, 2 nets.	300 yds east of the station. After Truro pass through two tunnels, over two viaducts and by Probus and Ladock Holt platform, fix on, run through Grampound Road station and by signal post, then lower and extend. 2 standards, 1 net.
23.	GOWERTON	575 yds. west of the station. Fix on at sidings, run through Gowerton station, under one bridge, over one bridge, then extend. 1 net.	Observe cutting, pass over river, at white signal board lower net. 1 standard. (1910)
24.	HAYES	578 yds. west of the station. Observe Southall station with sidings after, fix on, pass two bridges over canal, run through Hayes station and under bridge. At white signal board lower and extend. 1 standard, 1 net.	(No apparatus on the up journey)
25.	HAYLE		
26.	HEWISH	1¾ miles west of Yatton Station. After working Yatton fix on, observe Hewish level crossing and at white signal board extend. 1 net. (1924)	(No apparatus on the up journey)
27.	HIGHBRIDGE	250 yds. west of the station. Observe Brent Knoll station, fix on, run through Highbridge station and at the end of the platform lower and extend. 1 standard, 1 net.	550 yds. east of the station. Observe Dunball station, pass under 3 bridges, fix on, run through Highbridge station. At goods shed lower and extend. 1 standard, 1 net. (1924)
28.	HIGHWORTH JUNCTION		
29.	IVYBRIDGE	850 yds. east of the station. Observe Wrangaton station and Bittaford Halt platform, fix on, pass under 3 bridges, run by a signal post, at white signal board lower and extend. 1 standard, 1 net.	Pass Cornwood station, at side lines fix on, run through Ivybridge station and over viaduct, then lower and extend. 1 standard, 1 net.
30.	KIDWELLY	431 yds. west of station. Pass over river and under one bridge, fix on, run through station and over river bridge, then lower and extend. 1 standard, 1 net.	323 yds. west of station. After Ferry Side fix on, observe white board then lower and extend. 1 standard, 1 net.
31.	LANGFORD BRIDGE	1,000 yds. west of Newton Abbot apparatus. After working Newton Abbot fix on immediately, pass under one bridge and by Aller signal cabin, at white board extend. 1 net.	(No apparatus on the up journey.)
32.	LEOMINSTER	780 yds. north of station. Observe long tunnel, pass Ford Bridge station, notice side lines and goods shed, run through Leominster station and by level crossing gates, then lower net. 1 standard.	Observe 2 stations, fix on, pass under bridge and by 4 white gates, at white signal board extend. 1 net.
33.	LISKEARD	320 yds. west of the station. After Menheriot station pass over four viaducts, fix on, run through Liskeard station, at end of platform lower and extend. 1 standard, 1 net.	300 yds. west of the station. After Doublebois station pass under 3 bridges, notice cottages by side of the line, run over viaduct and by signal post, then lower and extend. 1 standard, 1 net.
34.	LLANTRISANT		

	LOCATION	DOWN JOURNEY	UP JOURNEY
35.	LLANSAMLET	260 yds. east of the station. Observe Skewen station, fix on, pass under one bridge, pass signal box, pass under six more bridges, at decline of cutting lower. 1 net.	170 yds. east of the station. After Landore Junction observe viaduct and tin works with furnaces, fix on, pass through station, at end of platform lower and extend. 1 standard, 1 net.
36.	LOSTWITHIEL	580 yds. west of the station. After Bodmin Road station observe side lines, fix on, pass through Lostwithiel station, over iron Fowey River bridge, then lower and extend. 1 standard, 1 net.	250 yds. east of station. After Par pass through tunnel, fix on, run through Lostwithiel station and by level crossing gates, then lower and extend. 1 standard, 1 net.
37.	LUDLOW	Observe 2 stations, run under 4 bridges and by a level crossing gate. Pass under 2 more bridges and at white signal board lower net. 1 standard.	98 yds. south of the station. Observe Onibury and Bromfield stations. At side lines fix on, run through Ludlow station and tunnel. Notice level crossing gate, pass over road bridge which has white railings, then extend. 1 net.
38.	LYDNEY JUNCTION	(No apparatus on the down journey)	420 yds. west of the station. After Chepstow, notice Woolaston station, pass under one bridge, at white signal board lower net. 2 standards. (1910)
39.	LOUGHOR	(No apparatus on the down journey)	365 yds. east of station. Pass over river, run through Loughor station and by platelayers hut, then lower net. 1 standard.
40.	MAIDENHEAD	620 yds. east of the station. Observe Taplow station, fix on, run over Thames bridge, pass parapet of next bridge, then lower and extend. 1 standard, 1 net. (1924)	350 yds. east of the station. After passing Twyford station notice Waltham sidings, fix on, run through Maidenhead station, at end of platform lower and extend. 1 standard, 1 net.
41.	MARAZION	605 yds. west of the station. After St. Erth station pass under two bridges, fix on, run through Marazion station and by two signal posts, then lower and extend. 1 standard, 1 net. (1924)	200 yds. east of the station. After Penzance observe Long Rock sidings, fix on, pass through Marazion station and by signal post, then lower and extend. 1 standard, 1 net. (1924)
42.	NAILSEA	250 yds. west of station. After working Bourton observe side lines, fix on, pass end of station, extend. 1 net.	
43.	NEWTON ABBOT	¾ mile west of the station. After Teignmouth notice sidings, at Newton Abbot station fix on, pass under one bridge then over road bridge with house at side, after passing first signal post lower and extend. 1 standard, 1 net.	(No apparatus on the up journey)
44.	NEWNHAM	214 yds. east of the station. After leaving Gloucester pass 2 stations, fix on, run over iron bridge and at white signal board extend. 1 net.	(No north-bound working apparatus)
45.	PAR		
46.	PERRANWELL		
47.	PENZANCE		

	LOCATION	DOWN JOURNEY	UP JOURNEY
48.	PLYMPTON	735 yds. west of the station. Observe Cornwood station, fix on, run through Plympton station and under two bridges, lower net, pass over small stream, then extend. 1 standard, 1 net.	400 yds. east of the station. After Plymouth observe Laira sidings and Tavistock Junction, fix on, run through Plympton station, by water tank at end of platform and after passing signal post lower net, pass small bridge over road, then extend. 1 standard, 1 net.
49.	READING		
50.	REDRUTH	1130 yds. west of the station. After working Scorrier fix on, run through Redruth station and over viaduct, pass under one bridge and by signal post, then lower and extend. 1 standard, 1 net.	Notice Carn Brea station and branch line, fix on, pass under two bridges and through cutting, at white signal board lower and extend. 1 standard, 1 net.
51.	SALTASH		
52.	SCORRIER	515 yds. west of the station Observe Chacewater station, at side lines fix on, pass through Scorrier station and over road bridge, then lower and extend. 1 standard, 1 net.	510 yds. west of the station. After passing Redruth station observe small cottage, pass over road and under 1 bridge, fix on, run through long cutting, at white signal board lower and extend. 1 standard, 1 net.
53.	SHRIVENHAM		
54.	SLOUGH	1,045 yds. east of the station. Observe Langley station, fix on, pass under three bridges and by two signal posts, at white signal board lower and extend. 1 standard, 1 net.	910 yards east of the station. Observe Taplow and Burnham Beeches stations, pass Hay Mill signal cabin, fix on, run through Slough station and under bridge at end of sidings, then lower and extend. 1 standard, 1 net.
55.	SOUTHALL	770 yds. east of station. After Hanwell station observe long viaduct, fix on, pass over iron girder bridge and low parapet of next bridge, then lower and extend. 2 standards, 1 net.	830 yds. east of station. Observe Hayes station at gas works, fix on, run through Southall station, under footbridge, and by signal cabin, then lower and extend. 1 standard, 1 net.

An interesting view of wayside apparatus, believed to be at Swindon. The postman has erected the net and is locking the standard with two pouches ready for collection. The signalman has a clear view of the exchange from his box, which, together with at least one signal, has been set back further from the lineside to allow the appropriate clearances for the coach apparatus. *Courtesy Railway Magazine*

	LOCATION	DOWN JOURNEY	UP JOURNEY
56.	STEVENTON		
57.	ST. AUSTELL	597 yds. east of the station. After Par station notice high chimney, fix on, pass over iron bridge and under two bridges, then lower and extend. 1 standard, 1 net.	415 yds. east of the station. Notice Burngullow station, pass over two viaducts, fix on, run through St. Austell station and under 1 bridge, at white signal board immediately beyond signal post lower and extend. 2 standards, 1 net.
58.	ST. CLEARS		
59.	ST. GERMAN'S	468 yds. west of the station. After Saltash station observe tunnel, fix on, pass over two viaducts through St. German's station and under one bridge, at white signal board lower and extend. 1 standard, 1 net.	365 yds. west of the station. Observe Menheniot station, pass over two viaducts and under eight bridges, fix on, at white signal board lower and extend. 1 standard, 1 net.
60.	SWINDON	2 miles east of the station. After passing Shrivenham station, observe two bridges, and 2 viaducts. After second, fix on, pass under three bridges, lower and extend. Apparatus near large platelayers hut. 2 standards, 1 net.	No description given.
61.	TAUNTON		
62.	TEIGNMOUTH	220 yds. east of the station. After Dawlish observe 5 short tunnels, fix on, pass two stone huts on sea front and at iron gate in sea wall lower and extend. 1 standard, 1 net.	500 yds. east of the station. After Newton Abbot observe row of houses, fix on, pass through Teignmouth station and under 3 bridges (the last two close together) then lower and extend. 1 standard, 1 net.

The 'up' wayside apparatus point at Teignmouth in 1903. This could be seen clearly from the sea wall walk, except when in use.
Collection R. S. Carpenter

	LOCATION	DOWN JOURNEY	UP JOURNEY
63.	TIVERTON JUNCTION	605 yds. west of the station. Observe Burlescombe station, pass under one bridge, fix on, run by side line through Tiverton Junction station and by goods shed, pass under one bridge, then extend. 1 net.	608 yds. west of the station. After working Cullompton fix on, pass under 3 bridges then lower and extend. 1 standard, 1 net.
64.	TOTNES	596 yds. west of the station. After Newton Abbot observe tunnel, at iron bridge over roadway fix on, pass over River Dart and through Totnes station, run under one bridge and by water tank, lower net, pass low parapet of small bridge with railings behind, then extend. 1 standard, 1 net.	640 yds. west of the station. After Brent observe tunnel, pass under 3 bridges, fix on, notice stone cutting, under four more bridges, at white signal board lower and extend. 1 standard, 1 net.
65.	TRURO		
66.	TWYFORD		
67.	WALLINGFORD ROAD	See Cholsey and Moulsford station	
68.	WANTAGE ROAD	300 yds. west of the station. After Steventon station observe bridge over small stream, fix on, run through Wantage Road station, at end of the platform lower and extend. 1 standard, 1 net. (1898)	(No apparatus worked in the up direction)
69.	WELLINGTON	1,150 yds. east of the station. Observe Norton Fitzwarren station, fix on, notice brickyard with tall chimneys, pass parapets of two small bridges then lower and extend. 1 standard, 1 net.	1,320 yds. east of the station. After Burlescombe station pass through long tunnel, observe factory, fix on, run through Wellington station and under two bridges, at white signal board lower and extend. 1 standard, 1 net.
70.	WEST DRAYTON	350 yds. west of the station. After Hayes station observe Dawley signal box, fix on, run under 2 bridges, through West Drayton station and over road bridge, pass signal box, then lower and extend. 1 standard, 1 net.	274 yds. east of the station. Observe Langley station, pass over river, fix on, run through West Drayton station and by signal box, then lower and extend. 1 standard, 1 net.
71.	WESTON JUNCTION	Apparatus at Weston Old Junction 2 ⅝ mile west of Puxton station. Observe Puxton station, pass under 3 bridges, fix on, under two bridges then lower and extend. 1 standard, 1 net.	Observe Bleadon and Uphill station, fix on, notice Weston loop lines, platelayers' cottages, at white signal board lower and extend. 3 standards, 1 net.
72.	WOOTTON BASSETT	(No apparatus on the down journey)	440 yds. east of station. After passing Dauntsey station, pass under 5 bridges, fix on at lines, pass through station and under bridge lower and extend. 1 standard, 1 net.
73.	YATTON	550 yds. west of the station. Pass through short tunnel, observe Flax Bourton and Nailsea stations, under two bridges, fix on, through Yatton station and by side lines, at white board lower and extend. 1 standard, 1 net.	500 yds. west of the station. Observe Puxton station and signal box, at Hewish level crossing fix on, pass over stream, at white signal board lower and extend. 2 standards, 1 net.

ADDITIONAL APPARATUS LOCATION NOTES

BRIDGWATER	Site finally cleared on 18th September 1968.
BRITON FERRY	The apparatus was resited at a point 210 yds. east of the station on 13th September 1913.
BURRY PORT	Down standard dismantled 23rd January 1907 along with up net.
CHIPPENHAM	9th August 1949 – third set of standards removed. 18th-20th Sept. 1962 – site cleared. 1 hut and timbers removed to Leighton Buzzard and erected there on 11th Oct. 1962. This is not the hut now at Didcot. 27th July 1965 – standards re-erected. 4th July 1970 – site finally cleared.
CHOLSEY BRIDGE	Known later as Cholsey and Moulsford.
CULLOMPTON	1st October 1945 – shelter hut destroyed by fire. 17th January 1962 – site finally cleared.
DAWLISH	1898 location on the down side was 250 yds. west of the station while there was no apparatus on the up side.
DIDCOT	Didcot originally had an apparatus point in 1876. One hundred years later the preserved apparatus point was set up in the Great Western Society's depot.
FERRYSIDE	Up standard dismantled 23rd January 1907.
HEWISH	The 1898 site was 1¼ miles east of the station near the church and school and consisted of a net and a standard.
HIGHBRIDGE	1898 site 600 yds. west of the station. 1 net and standard. No. 2 set was damaged in the early 1960s by a passing TPO and was replaced. 24th March 1968 – site finally cleared.
IVYBRIDGE	1898 site 750 yds. west of the station in both directions, consisting of a net and standard.
LISKEARD	11th August 1965 – site cleared.
MAIDENHEAD	1898 site 450 yds. east of the station on the down side while the up was 2½ miles west of the station. Both had a single net and standard. 7th April 1950 – the TPO damaged a ground signal close to the apparatus point. 1954–1964. The apparatus was moved on several occasions to accommodate track work.
MARAZION	1898 location on both the up and down was 440 yds. east of the station and consisted of a net and a standard.
SCORRIER	1898 location in the down direction was 369 yds. west of the station with a net and a standard. Up direction – in 1898 the carriage net had to be extended after the footbridge or it would foul the latter. Down direction – in 1898 the site was 600 yds. from the station.
SLOUGH	1898 site: Down 940 yds west of the station. 2 nets, 1 standard. Up 560 yds. west of the station. 1 net, 1 standard.
ST. GERMAN'S	1898 sites both 650 yds west of the station, 1 net and 1 standard.
SWINDON	Re-sited 30th July 1945. 28th July 1965 – site finally cleared.
TIVERTON JUNC.	1898 sites: Down 440 yds from the station. Up 400 yds from the station.
TOTNES	1898 site 880 yds west of the station. 24th August 1966 – site finally cleared.
WELLINGTON	1898 site 1320 yds. east of the station.
WESTON SUPER MARE	The apparatus in 1898 was 2½ miles from the Weston Post Office at Old Junction.

An interesting photograph taken on 11th September 1945 at the resited Swindon apparatus point. The TPO vehicle is one of the three Diagram L 21 coaches (Nos. 793-5) used between 11th and 14th September for apparatus testing. The coaches worked down on the 9.15 a.m. Paddington to Bristol (12.27 a.m.) and returned on the 5.30 p.m. Bristol to Paddington (8.30 p.m.). The following Monday, the 17th, the first post war TPO service was reintroduced from Paddington to Penzance using these three coaches only. The TPO van, possibly 793, and the following passenger brake van, are in wartime all brown livery. The apparatus had just been worked as the last traductor arm has not returned to its vertical position; the carriage net appears to have received at least two bags and two were despatched.

Of further interest and nearly out of the picture is the locomotive with its Hawksworth tender. This can only be one of three of the then brand new 'County' class 4–6–0s which had just begun to appear, either 1000, 1001 or 1002, which at that time were not fitted with nameplates.

Author's collection

Post Office

APPENDIX No. 4

PADDINGTON CONNECTIONS WITH THE POST OFFICE TUBE RAILWAY

In order to avoid the inevitable congestion in London, the Post Office built their own underground railway to speed the mails between the Eastern District office at Whitechapel and Paddington station via the main sorting offices. It was opened on 5th December 1927 and connected to the station platforms by means of a number of conveyors and chutes.

The majority of arriving mail was, and still is, handled on platforms 8-11. Eight hatches along No. 11 platform connect to a subway served by conveyor No. 5 (30 cwt maximum load). This feeds conveyor No. 6 (20 cwt maximum load) which also serves platforms 8 and 9 and in turn delivers letter bags to the Post Office's underground platform, below the Paddington District Office, via an inclined chute. An auxiliary conveyor for parcels bags, No. 5A (10 cwt maximum load) starts near the end of the same platform and feeds another conveyor No. 7, which runs alongside No. 6.

Mail from the Post Office railway is carried up to the 'lawn' of the main line station, near the site of the former booking office, by two conveyors, No. 8 for letter bags and No. 9 for parcels (both with a 40 cwt maximum load). On reaching the lawn, the bags are taken to the appropriate platform on both railway and Post Office owned platform trolleys.

Conveyors and chutes are also in use at Mount Pleasant, King Edward Building, Liverpool Street station and at the Western, West Central and Eastern Post Offices.

The 'Lawn' arrival point of conveyor No. 9 at Paddington with a number of bags having arrived from the Post Office underground railway. *Post Office*

A Mercury tractor towing two GWR platform trolleys away from conveyor No. 8 to an awaiting train on 26th October 1949. *Post Office*

Plan showing the arrangement of the tracks and conveyors of the Post Office Tube Railway at Paddington station.

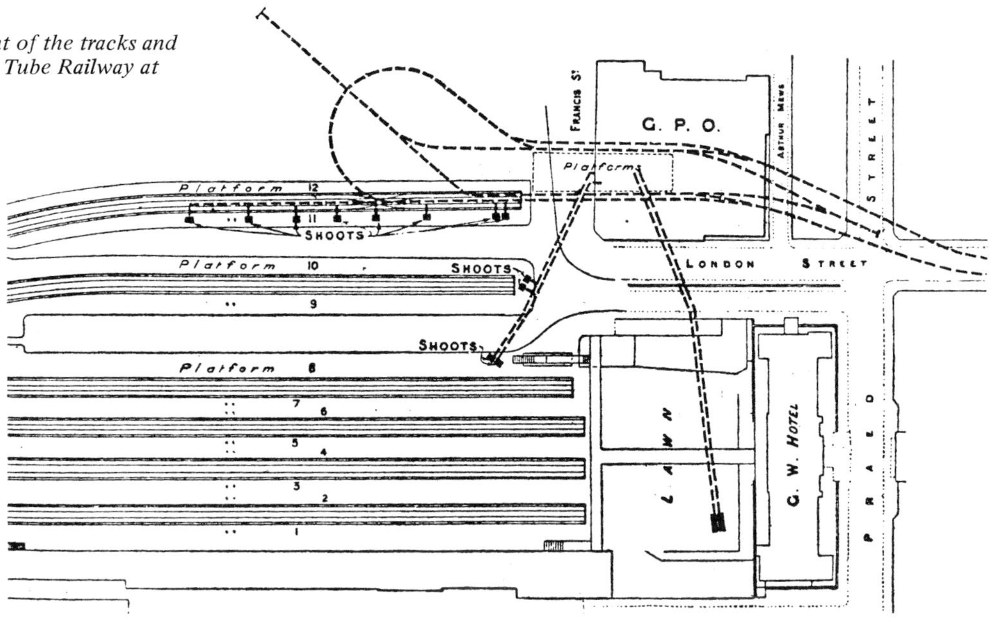

The open space of the 'Lawn' is useful for the handling of mail. This view shows mail being offloaded from two 1946 Morris 30 cwt vans of the LC series onto standard GWR station barrows. *Post Office*

The exchange of mail bags can still be seen at Didcot Railway Centre, Oxfordshire, using the preserved Great Western TPO Stowage Van No. 813. *British Railways*

ACKNOWLEDGEMENTS

Information for this book has proved somewhat elusive, partly because the majority of the operation occurs at night and partly due to Post Office security, which in turn has helped to create the mystique surrounding the TPOs.

The seeds of my own interest were sown when contemplating the preservation of one of the redundant GWR TPO coaches. After various abortive attempts, No. 814 was eventually secured and enquiries began into its past history and the whole TPO operation. This book has resulted from my research, but ironically the exact date of the original No. 814 has yet to be established!

I would like to thank first the Manager of the Travelling Post Office Section and Mr. Dennis Clark, who have made information available from their own sources. I should also like to thank the Post Office's own library, record room and photographic section; the National Postal Museum; the Public Record Office; numerous people from British Railways at Swindon, Paddington and Eastleigh, and the British Transport Docks Board for help with the Ocean Mails story.

Of the large number of individuals who have also helped, I would particularly like to thank Mr. W. Beard, Jack Crawley, Jane Criddle, D. Cross, V. Day, P. English, P. Garland, D. Geen, Fred Gray of the Great Western Society, D. J. Hyde, J. Hodgetts, G. B. Jones, P. Jones, J. Lewis, M. M. Lloyd, Captain E. Madgewick, Eric Mountford, S. O'Connell and R. P. Walford.

For the production of the book I would like to extend special thanks to Peter Webber for reading the manuscript, Paul Karau and June Judge.